ETHEL

The Letter

Jan Dixon

Knockland Press

For Caitlin, David, William and Victoria

PREFACE

The spoils of war oft times come back to haunt.

A rifle shot resounds through the rain forest in the South Westland area of South Island New Zealand. A helicopter lands on a nearby stoney beach to rescue an injured man. Twenty years before an airmail letter arrives in Christchurch from Scotland, all linked - but how. Jealousy and hatred follow, and revenge it seems is seldom sweet.

CHAPTER 1

New Zealand 1986

Past Connections

The airmail letter from the United Kingdom arrived in early September, spring, the start of the whitebait season on the west coast of South Island. The usual preparations were underway for the trip to the Paringa river, where Hector and his wife Cath live in their *bach* till the end of the season in November. He had built their river home with his own hands, using wood from the rain forest which lay along the banks of the river, one of many which flowed into the Tasman Sea. The narrow coastal area along this southern part of South Island was wedged between the sea and the Southern Alps. Access to the bach was either by jetboat or trekking, and in emergencies, by helicopter. Simple as their accommodation was, they had their own generator, CB radio, wood stove, simple homemade shower, two canoes, and a quadbike. The main equipment they needed was the white baiting stands and nets, a couple of rifles kept in a locked gun cabinet, a rainwater vat and the usual household goods for their simple everyday needs, with a supply of candles for darker evenings and early mornings. Fresh provisions were regularly brought down by the water bailiff Tom Connal, who was in radio contact daily. Living only five miles upstream at the bridge, where the main highway, Route 6 from Nelson to Queenstown and beyond to Invercargill, crossed the Paringa.

Gathering the last few things together, extra towels and personal items through in the bedroom, Cath never heard the doorbell. Instead, it was Hector, coming out of the double garage after filling up the car's washer bottle, checking the oil level and tyre pressures, who met the postman. Thanking him, before shoving the letter in his trouser pocket, saying that was them nearly ready for moving over to the coast.

'Yes, it is that time again,' Hector said, 'seems to come round quicker every year. Just put our mail through the letter box as usual, our son brings it down the coast when he visits. Anyway, we'll catch up in a couple of months' time on our return.'

'Unusual, an airmail letter from the United Kingdom, never noticed you getting one before?' the postman noted.

Hector, wiping his hand on his trousers, brought the letter out of his pocket. 'Yip,' he reacted, as he turned to go into the house, 'unusual, sure is.'

Waiting till he was inside with the door closed, before studying the envelope prior to opening it. He sat at the table by the window, where it was lighter, and started reading the neat, hand written letter. His heart rate increasing with every word, the beat loud, his mind not quite believing. He held the letter close, trying to take it all in. Cath coming through from the back of the house and seeing Hector sitting at the table, stepped forward and looked at the envelope. Not recognising the writing, yet noticing his trembling hand,

'What's this?' she queried, looking at the sender's address. Then taking the letter out of his hand, 'Who's this?' after reading the first few lines, her face reddening, a mixture of anger and disbelief. 'Who is this, I said?'

Not getting up, but stretching over to try to take the letter back out of her hand, saying, 'Please Cath, give me the letter, it has nothing to do with you. Us, I mean.'

'Then who has it to do with?' she shouted. 'Who is she? What does she want?

'Please just give me the letter and I'll explain.'

'Explain, explain, yes, you had better explain. Is this from a daughter? You have a daughter? Where is she? Who is she? Why is she writing to you? Why now? Where is she, why haven't you told me before? After all this time and you have never said a word about having a daughter. Why? Why? Why?'

Sobbing, and sounding desperate. Getting louder and louder, before collapsing into the armchair still clutching the letter. Then repeating slowly and clearly, 'Yes, you had better explain.'

Swivelling round in his chair to look at Cath, he replied, 'Yes, I have a daughter, I do, and I am sorry. No, I am not sorry, but sorry you had to find out this way.'

'Well, I know now, so what have you to say?'

'Nothing. I don't know. There has never been a right moment. It was all a long time ago. Years before we met. I didn't even know where she was, never did. It was towards the end of the war, early 1945. The war ended in May, then in August I was sent back to the Pacific and I never saw her again. There has never been a right moment Cath, please believe me, please understand.'

'Understand? How can I understand? You have lied to me all these years, and anyway, how did she know who you are and where you are? Why suddenly contact you now?'

'I don't know,' Hector wearily replied. 'I don't know. Please just give me the letter.'

'No.'

'Please Cath,' he repeated, keeping eye contact.

Reluctantly handing the letter over she sat back down burying her face in her hands and sobbed.

Getting up she fumbled in a pocket for a hankie to wipe her tear-stained face as she stumbled through to the bedroom, slamming the door. The crying stopped; all was quiet. Hector taking his time read the letter several times, smoothing out each page on the table, hardly able to believe his eyes.

It was then Hector heard another door close in the narrow hallway, they had been overheard. Both forgetting in the heat of the moment they were not alone, every word, every cross, accusing word, and admission, had been heard. Neil, her son, his step-son, had been listening, overhearing everything.

CHAPTER 2

South Island - New Zealand 1998

The Shooting.

In the shadow of Mount Cook and Mount McFarlane in the Southern Alps, the Paringa river, flows west from Lake Paringa to empty into the Tasman Sea, with the Haast River to the south, and Fox Glacier to the north. Along the coastline were old gold workings and gold fields. Whilst deer culling in the Southern Alps in the 1950s, Hector and his friend and team mate Alan Rodgers discovered a small gold seam in one of the rain forest's covered valleys above the Paringa. Now forty years later, having organised a helicopter flight from Hokitika, complete with backpack, a tent, billycan and provisions Hector set off full of hope. Realising two days later he had been a bit foolhardy and that the whole trip had been foolish and wishful thinking, he decided to have one last search before packing up and heading out as planned, no richer, but certainly wiser. No fool like an old fool - how true.

As the gun shot echoed across the river and around the valley, there was a complicated mix of the tuneful notes, coughs, grunts and wheezes of the black looking, white throated tui birds, startled into noisy, whirring, fast flight along with the forked tail bell birds, whose thousands of tiny whistles and flutes rose high above the forest canopy. Iridescent cool blue, bronze and olive-green feathers caught on the branches, soon softly floated down to the earth in the now silent valley.

Hearing the shot from across the Paringa, local west coaster,

Wayne Kelly, out enjoying a spot of late afternoon fishing, hoping to catch a trout for dinner, looked up, puzzled. Peering across from the south bank to where he thought the gun shot had come, Wayne caught sight of a man edging down out of the bush, stumble along the stoney river bank and disappear through a gap in the thick undergrowth. Within minutes he re-appeared on a quadbike, its engine gunning as he sped along the pebbly beach. Perhaps sensing he was being watched, he turned sharply towards the higher bush covering, hitting a washed-up tree stump. Quadbike and rider were airborne, then as if in slow motion, landing on the rough stony sand, the bike falling heavily on the awkwardly sprawled, still figure.

Shocked into action, Wayne crashed out of the water, dropped his rod, catching his breath as he ran along the pebbly beach to his bach, to call the Search and Rescue Service Centre at Hokitika on his Citizens Band radio. Breathlessly, he reported what he had seen, and where. Repeating carefully what Wayne had told her, the operator assured him help would be with him soon. Wayne thought it best to also call the river bailiff, Tom Connal, to report the accident. Tom's home, office and storage outhouses were five miles upstream, where the west coast Route 6 from Nelson to Invercargill bridged the Paringa. Setting off right away, Wayne soon heard Tom's jet boat approaching the beach on the north side opposite, followed not long after by the sound of the incoming rescue helicopter. Having landed, the helicopter crew, with their rescue gear and stretcher, were quickly clear of the rotor blades and running towards Tom, standing by the trapped motionless body.

High in the forest the tuis and bellbirds had settled, the raucous calling now silent. Coming to, Hector was aware of pain in his upper left arm, along with a throbbing ache in the back of his head, having fallen awkwardly on to a piece of rock with the impact and shock of the sudden attack. Struggling to raise himself up onto his right elbow, he blacked out. Shortly he was roused by the noise of a helicopter engine and whirring blades.

Realising that it was still daylight, though having lost all idea of time, he was thankful that help had come. His mind however started spin like the blades. Who knew he was here, who knew what had happened, heard or even saw who had tried to shoot him? Growing weaker and colder, he slipped once more into oblivion.

On the beach, the young man trapped beneath the quad bike was also drifting in and out of consciousness. The doctor finding his legs had little pulse and no response to touch, administered painkillers, allowing the team to remove the bike. Eventually lifting him on to the stretcher with great care, they carried him along the beach to the waiting helicopter. Radioing ahead the pilot was advised to fly to Greymouth Hospital, where a medical team would assess the casualty. The accident would also be reported to the police at Greymouth, in case of foul play.

After thanking the rescue team, Tom. watched them manoeuvre the injured man into the helicopter, before returning to drag the quadbike, with difficulty, further back up the stony beach to keep it clear of the early morning high tide. Walking over to his jetboat Tom waved across to Wayne, who had been patiently watching the proceedings and final dramatic rescue. Starting up the engine Tom headed across the river to bring Wayne up to date. It seemed the younger man had seriously injured his spine, the worst scenario, along with other minor injuries. Tom also wanted to pass on the rescue team's thanks to Wayne for his quick thinking in alerting them so promptly.

He told Tom he had heard a gunshot not long before the joker had appeared out of the rain forest. Tom replied that no gun had been found at the rescue scene.

'Oh well, maybe shooting possum,' Wayne added, knowing the bother the creatures were, consuming birds' eggs, chicks, and eating up to half a pound of new growth of foliage every day. So yea, he thought, shooting possum was fair game.

He also thanked Tom for coming down the river so sharply and helping the Rescue Team, as he had felt pretty helpless watching from the other bank. Tom smiled and nodded, as he turned and walked back over to his jet boat. Climbing in he switched on, shouting back over the noise of the engine, 'Wayne, I'll check old Hec's place to see if there is any sign of life. Catch you later.'

Strange though he thought to himself, I haven't heard from him or his step son recently. As he manoeuvred the boat over to the other bank he had a feeling he had recognised the injured fellow, though hadn't said anything. Remembering too it was a couple of months ago the joker's mother had died suddenly, and neither he nor his step father had been down the river since. Scrambling up the rough beach to have a quick look round, confirmed there was no sign of life at the bach. Soon heading back home up the river as the sun slipped lower behind him in the western sky over the Tasman Sea, his mind mulling over the tragic events of the afternoon.

Beaching his jetboat, he then dragged it up towards the boathouse before tidying and sorting his equipment ready for the following morning. Heading across the grass and up the path to the front door of his corrugated-iron roofed wooden house, his first thought was to make himself a much-needed mug of tea, adding a dash of the amber nectar. Checking his radio messages next to see if there was any news regarding the injured man, but no, nothing. Tom settled down in his chair to ponder over the happenings of the afternoon and enjoy his hot drink. Later as promised he called Wayne to talk over the day's events, but mainly to see if he was alright. You kept an eye out for one another in this remote part of the world.

Dusk was falling, the air chilling fast, creeping into and around every inch of Hector's bruised and wounded body. He knew he must try and reach his simple shelter before dark, drink some water, and try to patch himself up as best he could. It wasn't the first time he had been in this Alpine wilderness injured, many years before killing and butchering a deer had nearly cost him a leg. Remembering too, in 1942, on HMS Achilles, the Japanese had tried and failed, so an off the mark rifle shot, he could survive, he was sure.

CHAPTER 3

South Island – New Zealand

Ethel and James

1920s

On the front page of the *Nelson Evening Mail* of Saturday 2nd February 1924, in the *Wanted Column* between '*6 hop pickers wanted by the end of February, apply Drogemuller, Upper Moutere*' and '*Married couple want work, apply, J Greenhill, Brightwater*' was '*Wanted – a kind lady to adopt a healthy baby boy, 2 weeks old, apply 5 Washington Road, Nelson.*

Ethel and James, working on their farm in the Dovedale settlement overlooking Golden Bay in the Tasman District of New Zealand's upper South Island, had settled down for the evening after dinner. Having read what interested him in the evening paper James passed it over to Ethel, who, putting her sewing down, glanced over the front page columns. Laying the paper down, she went through to the kitchen to put the kettle on the wood stove to make them both a fresh pot of tea. The warm tea, a hard day's work in the summer sun along with cosy camaraderie, soon lulled Robert into a light sleep. Picking up the paper and glancing over at her sleeping husband Ethel smiled to herself. Her eye was drawn to an advert in the *Wanted* column, - *kind lady wanted to adopt a healthy baby boy*. She gasped. James stirring slightly, mumbled incoherently then drifted off again. Ethel watching him, didn't want to wake him, not yet anyway.

The address was well known to her, and would have been to James too, had he spotted it. It was their son's address in Nelson.

He and his wife had had a baby boy in the spring, so what could this mean? Only one thing, and Ethel knew there had been rumours. Trying to ignore them during the tea break at the church guild meetings, or in the local store, she most certainly had never discussed it with James. Ethel knew deep down, the baby boy must also be her grandson, James's too. Somehow, she would try to convince her husband they could give the boy a home.

Ethel knew, even though being in her fifties, she was still fit and healthy. Besides she couldn't face the thought of her own grandson being given away to strangers. She and James had been working on the farm since he returned at the end of the war, their family was well in their twenties now, married and leading their own lives. Their son Colin and his wife lived in Nelson, and had a baby boy, Robert. and daughter Mavis had a young family, and living not far away in a wooden homestead near Dovedale.

James now 57 years old, had been one of the 1,400 men, a small volunteer force raised in New Zealand shortly after the outbreak of World War 1. Samoa, at that time, was of moderate strategic importance to Germany. The radio transmitter located in the hills above Apia was capable of sending long range Morse signals to Berlin, and able too, to communicate with the 90 warships in Germany's naval fleet. Apia is located on the central north coast of Upolu, Samoa's second largest island. A harbourside town, an 18th century colonial style municipality, which in the late 1950s became the capital.

When war broke out in Europe on 4th August 1914, Britain asked New Zealand to seize German Samoa as a *'great and urgent Imperial service'* and New Zealand's response was swift. The Samoa Advance Party of the Expeditionary Force landed at Apia on 29th August some three weeks or so later. There was no opposition, as German Samoa had no soldiers or military hardware and surrendered almost immediately. The Union Jack was hoisted above the Apia Courthouse, and New Zealand ruled Samoa for the next 48 years. The Samoans, a Polynesian people, closely related to the native Māoris of New Zealand, had first migrated there due to work opportunity as far back as the 1870s. James, now 51 years, came home safely after the end of the war, unlike many thousands of his fellow countrymen, and adapted thankfully and quickly into the farming life again.

Ethel waiting her moment to tell her husband about her idea, hoping he would agree, then it would be a joint decision. Their small farm in Dovedale near Golden Bay seemed an ideal place to bring up a young boy, of this Ethel was sure.

CHAPTER 4

Young Ethel

Late 1880s – 1924

As James dozed peacefully in his chair, Ethel, enjoying this quiet time together too, let her mind drift back thirty-five years or so. She was only eighteen, living and working in Taranaki, North Island, and finding herself in a similar position to Hector's birth mother, pregnant, with no husband.

Along with one of her sisters and several brothers they were living and working in the region during the season of cheese making and lambing. Along with other general farm work, many of the young folks moved around as the seasons changed. It was all mainly cyclical work, so, it was normal to move back to South Island for the seasonal picking and packing of berries, apples, hops and kiwi fruit, with the young men moving back to work in and around the Nelson dock area.

Realising her difficulty, Ethel remembered that after talking to her sister, she decided it would be best if she moved away from the community of Taranaki to have her baby. Planning on going to Wellington by train, then taking the ferry over to Picton on South Island. Their parents were still living in the Dovedale area of Nelson where Ethel herself had been born, in Ranzau, a settlement founded by immigrant German families in 1844. Gathering together what she thought she would need into a case; she said a tearful goodbye to her sister, and promising to keep in touch, she headed off to New Plymouth station with one of the young farmhands in his horse and cart.

Settling on the train, and taking time to look around her, she recognised a young man Ernest, about her own age, she smiled as he caught her eye. Coming over he asked if he could sit beside her, agreeing and easing over to make room for him, they soon started talking. Learning from his easy conversation that he too was planning on going to South Island, having family in and around the Nelson area, as Ethel had. Sounding like a good opportunity to Ethel, and with Ernest seeming keen, both decided to go to Wellington together.

On the hundred and fifty-nine-mile journey Ethel explained her situation, Ernest was intrigued, suggesting rather boldly that her baby would have his name if they got married, also that it might be easier to find work as a married couple. It could work out well for both of them, and the baby. After arriving in Wellington and finding a room to rent without too much trouble, the couple set about finding a church with a minister willing to marry them. All went to plan, with Ethel and Ernest quietly married before moving back to Dovedale a few months later, after baby Eva was born. The year was 1889, the month September. Married in haste, however they didn't have long to repent, as they divorced a few years later. After many years on her own, in 1901 Ethel met and married James, by this time her daughter Eva was thirteen. Several months later Eva had a baby brother Colin, Ethel's second child, followed by a daughter Mavis. All now grown up, and married with families of their own.

The Nelson Tasman region Dovedale is part of, enjoys a moderate maritime climate, enjoying some of the highest hours of sunshine in the whole country. The spring months of September, October and November bring much needed rain for the crops, with milder temperatures of 60-66 degrees as the days start to lengthen. December, January and February, summer in Abel Tasman, becomes sub-tropical, with children and young people running barefoot, playing on nearby beaches, swimming, or rummaging and foraging through the bush, with the added excitement of Christmas and the school holidays. The mellow months of autumn, March, April and May, still mild enough for swimming and outdoor games, is quickly followed by the crisp, clear mornings of winter, June, July and August. Usually sunny by lunchtime, still with enough daylight to be able to play outside after school. In the evenings after dinner, homework, and before bedtime a story by a warm, wood fire. Ethel felt their new grandson would enjoy an idyllic childhood on the farm, learning about cows, sheep and hens, from herself and Robert his new mother and father.

Ethel put the suggestion to James a couple of days later while sitting together on the wooden porch looking out over the summer pasture in the warm evening light. James was convinced. Replying to the advert, Ethel was pleased to receive a prompt reply in return and started making arrangements to collect the precious package in Nelson. The reply asked her to be at the house a couple of doors down from number 5, and it was there she would be able to collect the baby boy a week later. Ethel started gathering together items she knew she would need. A small cradle, blankets, baby feeding bottles, towelling nappies, and pleased too that both her daughters were as excited and able to give her 'hand me down' baby clothes, with one daughter even managing to find a pram stored away at the back of one of their wooden sheds. Soon the older 'new' parents were organised.

The following Tuesday afternoon, both anxious and nervous, they set off for Nelson in the farm truck. Dropping Ethel off a few doors further down Washington Road, James sat and waited. Walking along the road to number 9 she rang the bell. Standing back anxiously, she could hear scuffling and a young child crying, as the door was opened the door. A dark haired, attractive woman, in her late thirties at least, stepped forward, holding the baby. She looked as if she too had been crying. A little boy, of about three, with rosy cheeks and a head of curly, golden curls, clutched tightly on to his mother's skirt, sobbing. Smiling, Ethel stepped forward to gently pat the little boy, which made him cry even louder. Letting go his mother's skirt he ran back into the house. Dolly now even more distressed handed baby Hector over. Ethel tried reassuring her that she would take great care of her baby and if she wished she would keep in touch occasionally, letting her know of his progress. Ethel smiled holding Hector close, but with little else to say both turned away, one back into the house where she lived and worked as a housekeeper, to try and comfort her other young son Doug, and Ethel back along the road with her new precious bundle to James. Taking a few moments to look and admire their new baby son, he smiled at Ethel, shaking his head gently before the new wee family headed back to Dovedale, to bring up their newly adopted son, their grandson.

As Ethel had predicted, Hector's young life was indeed idyllic. As soon as he could walk, he followed after Ethel everywhere. Scattering grain for the hens, and hunting around the hidden corners in the yard every day for freshly laid eggs. Watching amazed, as Ethel milked their cow, also helping to hang out the washing by handing his mother the wooden clothes pegs, and eventually helped with weeding the vegetable garden. He enjoyed running about after the few sheep they had, who never really wandered far from the homestead, even coming when he called their names, they were more like pets. Like most boys his age however, his greatest wish was to be big enough to sit up in the tractor beside his father and work in the fields.

By 1929, when he was five years old, Hector started at the rural, wooden, white painted, Dovedale school, which had opened in 1869 the year Ethel had been born. Walking to school in the mornings, then home again in the afternoons by himself was exciting for a young boy, lots of things to see, to do, to collect, a wonderland for a young mind. Hector was soon settling in, making friends and enjoying most of the early lessons. The sun shone, the little family were busy and happy, admitting many times that Ethel's idea of adopting and bringing up their grandson had been a good idea, ideal.

CHAPTER 5

North Island – South Island - New Zealand

Mid 1800s - Family Emigrations Remembered

Remembering the dramatic volcanic cone of Mount Taranaki in North Island, seemed far from Ethel's life in Dovedale now. First seen by the British navigator James Cook and his crew in January 1770, as they sailed south off the Raglan coast into the North Taranaki Bight at the edge of the Tasman Sea. It reminded Cook of Mount Teide, the volcano on Tenerife in the Canary Islands, Spain, the highest point above sea level in the islands of the Atlantic Ocean. A few days later sailing off the future site of New Plymouth, Cook named the mountain Mount Egmont, after the Earl of Egmont, First Lord of the Admiralty.

It was less than a century later, with the influx of European settlers in Taranaki creating a demand for farmland, more than was available, that Ethel's grandmother and family, and James's grandfather arrived in New Zealand. The fertile volcanic lands around the Mountain were ideal for farming and soon the area was surrounded by dairy and sheep farms, and to the west by the beaches and sweeping surf of the Tasman Sea. Though in the 1860s *Māori* opposition to land purchases by European immigrants led to conflict throughout this time in the *Parihaka* community, in the Taranaki region. The original forests of the Taranaki ring plain were mostly cleared and turned into pasture, though a farsighted decision in 1881 declared the land within the radius of the mountain was made a forest reserve, preserving the timber resource for years to come.

Ethel recalled hearing her father James Winn, talk of his long sea voyage from England when he was a boy. At the age of thirteen, Colin, along with his older brother William, mother Elizabeth and new stepfather, arrived in Port Nelson, South Island, New Zealand, aboard the *Thomas Harrison* at the end of October 1842, having left Portsmouth England on May 25th before spending six long weeks becalmed in the tropics. A long sea voyage indeed, and to an unknown destination. Having at last crossed the Tasman Sea and sighting land at Cape Farewell, the north west tip of South Island, the barque rounded Farewell Spit, sailing on down through Golden Bay on into Tasman Bay at the head of which lay their final destination, the haven of Nelson.

On the morning of Tuesday 26th October, the ship was greeted with cheers by industrious European settlers hard at work building ships at the port, also around the shores of Tasman Bay, where the timber used for the ships grew and was felled. Only discovered by Europeans the previous year, and formerly known as the Haven by *Māoris*, it was the spawning ground for the fish, red snapper. Vessels now came in with the tide and went out against it. The Haven entrance was narrow, though sufficiently deep in the harbour. Many ships became stranded at the mouth of the Haven in the early days.

Seven months before the *Thomas Harrison* sailed in to the Haven, the immigrant ship *Fifeshire*, continuing on with its maiden voyage to Macao in China, drifted due to light wind upon the Arrow rock at the narrow entrance to the Haven, was broken in two and totally wrecked. So it was that many had long given up hope of the *Thomas Harrison's* safe arrival. Therefore, the excitement grew as the passengers and the crowd watched the large vessel edge closer and closer to the wharf, under the expertise of the pilot. In spite of the long tedious journey and the death of two children, the immigrants loudly cheered their captain, Captain Smith, for their safe deliverance to New Zealand.

Ethel's grandmother Elizabeth a widow, originally from

Wiltshire, her two young sons, new husband Mr Roberts and baby daughter born in New Zealand, lived in and around the Nelson area. When they were young men Elizabeth's sons William, and his brother John, Ethel's father, put their money together and became the first settlers in Dovedale on the River Dove. The river rising in the Tekoa Range, between the Wai-iti River and the Motueka River, flowed north west into the Motueka River near the locality of Woodstock, named after the native New Zealand pigeons, found in the forests around the river. William and John transformed this bush land into profitable farm land. Grass lands with flocks of sheep, herds of cattle, along with fields of grain, surrounding the slowly increasing habitations with small wooden farmsteads. Soon more new immigrants settled into their new way of life in Dovedale, thousands of miles from their old homeland.

Ethel, remembering too that James's father also emigrated to New Zealand in the 1840s, travelling from Scotland. Also called James, and originally from Thankerton, Lanarkshire, had left the family home to seek a new life in New Zealand. James in due course met and married Emily, whose father Emanuel, a farmer and tutor, later became the editor of the Nelson Evening Mail. Emanuel had sailed out to New Zealand from Portsmouth dock in February 1845 on the barque *Slains Castle*, taking with him a library of books, two French doors and 4000 gold coins. The *Slains Castle,* named after an old castle in Aberdeenshire, in north east Scotland, overlooked the epeiric North Sea, from its cliff top site on *Cruden Bay*. The Castle was famous for many reasons, one being that in the 19th century many notable people were entertained there including Bram Stoker, leading to the belief that *Slains Castle* was the inspiration for the setting of Count Dracula in 1897.

Emanuel met his young wife Emma, a teacher from Yorkshire, and they settled in Stanley Brook, in Dovedale, both ideal pioneers in their new country. The Ebans raised a large family, with Emma teaching in the local school, and Emanuel furthering the awareness of local, district and national news with the expansion of the Nelson Newspaper. Living on their farm and providing employment for local workers, ingratiated them to many families, especially those with young men looking for work locally.

Now it seemed to Ethel that the family had another connection to the Ebans as Hector's adoption advert had been placed in the Nelson Evening Mail, and towards the end of World War 11, Ethel would again be grateful to the newspaper for publishing a telegraph communication from her son somewhere in the waters around Northern Europe, letting her know he was safe and well. In her mind it all seemed to tie up as the generations continued to grow around the Nelson, Dovedale area.

CHAPTER 6

Dovedale to Nelson

Earthquake and Death

1929 - 30

Ethel's older daughter Eva rented a farm every year at *Puramahoi*, a coastal property on Golden Bay. She and her family came down from Taranaki on North Island's west coast, during the cheese making off season. The sons worked at the *Onekaka* iron works, also tackling some of the heavier work on the farm, while the girls were mostly involved in fruit picking and apple packing. The boys all played rugby, so Ethel made a point of helping Eva wash the boys' rugby kits in the stream which flowed passed the property. On one busy morning Ethel called on Hector, who was playing nearby, to bring her some more soap. Running happily to the house to help his mother, he was soon back out having found a fresh bar of soap. Reaching the stream, he knelt down beside Ethel as he handed her the soap, and at that same moment the earth shook violently, with a thundering noise filling the air.

The Murchison Earthquake struck on the morning of the 17th of June 1929.

Ethel quickly grabbed young Hector drawing him close to her as she lay on the ground protecting him with her body as the rumbling increased. The stream rising quickly, was now full of thick mud. Holding closely on to one another, there followed a loud crashing sound as the chimney fell into Eva's farmstead. The tremors continued. The earth shuddering, boulders, mud and debris rolling down the hillside, through the thick bush area. Luckily, the most intense shaking occurred in the mountainous, densely wooded areas, which were fortunately sparsely populated, so casualties were therefore comparatively light, with the damage mostly confined to the surrounding landscape. However, the shaking triggered extensive landslides over thousands of square kilometres and the shock impacted with damaging results as far away as Nelson, Cape Farewell and Greymouth on the West coast, with the massive rumblings heard as far away as New Plymouth on North Island. The aftershocks trailed on for several months across the region, with some as far north as Takaka, and around the homesteads near Golden Bay.

Soon the family gathered together, relieved that no one was injured. They rallied round to sort out as best they could the damage inside and outside of Eva's steading. Ethel and James's farm had escaped fortunately with no damage to their property. Everyone was safe, which was the main concern. The Shaky Isles yet again living up to its name.

Unexpectedly three months later in September 1930 James died.

Deciding it would be better to send Hector to stay with her son Colin's family in Nelson till after James's funeral, Ethel misguidedly thought it would be like staying with family, and so it was quickly arranged. They had a young son Robert the same age, so Hector would have young company, and for a few weeks he would be able to go to school in Nelson with Robert, which Ethel felt would help Hector cope with the loss of his father. Soon realising she couldn't stay on in the farm, Ethel didn't know what was going to happen to them? It would be too much work for her on her own, and she couldn't afford to employ a full-time farm hand.

Regrettably, Ethel did have to come out of the farm, it was as she thought, she could no longer afford the lease the farmstead or work the farm herself. Soon after the funeral, and the sorting out of all the paperwork relating to the farm completed, she moved in with her daughter Mavis. Living not too far away in a small *rimu* wood dwelling, bordering the edge of a large field under the watchful eye of Mount Arthur, which like Mount Taranaki, the tops were covered in snow, both winter and spring.

The change from living on the farm to living in Nelson was a big leap for young Hector, he not only missed his father, but especially his mother. This was his first experience of death, and he was struggling to understand. He felt lost and alone. He cried himself to sleep most nights, which annoyed Colin's wife, who had little feeling for the young Hector, who himself had no understanding that Colin was really his father, and not a much older brother. He so wanted to be back with Ethel, to have her hug him and say everything would be fine and would soon back to normal. But of course, it wouldn't.

The days turned into weeks, the weeks into months, and still Hector was living with his step mother and half-brother Robert. His birth father Colin who drove a taxi in town, was away often, travelling. He was a choir master, regularly crossing from Picton on the ferry to Wellington on North Island to conduct choirs. During these long weeks away from Ethel and home, Hector was punished for crying long into the night, and at times wetting the bed which only made things worse. Colin's wife took her anger out on Hector when he was away, thrashing him; that it was with unbelievable joy, when Ethel eventually arrived to collect Hector and take him home. He ran into her arms both laughing and crying with unbelievable relief.

Hector's freedom and joy at being back with his mother softened the blow of not returning to the farm at Golden Bay. Instead, they moved in with Ethel's daughter Mavis and her young son Roddie, to their small homestead. Again, as in Golden Bay there was plenty of open space for the boys to run about, chasing one another, playing with the dogs, gathering eggs and helping to milk their one cow. The two youngsters were happy in each other's company, with Hector settling in to his old school again, which was only brisk walk from the homestead. Meeting up with his school friends, and being with Ethel, his young life was happy once again.

After school, the boys and some of their friends played cricket and their own version of rugby, at other times they enjoyed guddling for fish in the streams, fed by the melting snow, it kept the boys busy, happy, and out of mischief. Though mischief was usually in their minds when the minister called, always seeming, to the boys anyway, to over stay his welcome. He made no secret of enjoying the home baking, rarely refusing a second helping of cake with his warm sweet tea. The young boys enjoyed playing tricks on the frequent visitor, sneaking back outside when the adults were chatting. They harnessed his old horse to his cart through the fence, sometimes even managing to face the horse into the cart. Such fun was enjoyed from a safe distance, as they watched the older man struggle to leave after dark, with both boys giggling and running back home out of the way before he spotted them. The pranks never seemed to bother the minister too much, as his fondness for home baking and female company outstripped any annoyance. Or perhaps he grasped if he said nothing, the boys would hopefully tire of their mischief.

ss

CHAPTER 7

Top House Murder Connection

1894

Not only in 1930 did Ethel's husband James die, her first husband Ernest died too. She hadn't heard from him for quite some time, though over the years he did occasionally contact her to ask about their daughter Eva. Eva herself, not remembering Ernest, had no contact with him and Ethel had never found it necessary to mention him. Eventually however he let Ethel know he had moved to North Island to Glen Eden, a suburb of West Auckland. Never remarrying he had lived a quiet life, and Ethel in due course learnt he had died and was buried in the cemetery in Glen Eden, so far away, she remembered from where he had been born, in Gloucester, England. Far too, from the Nelson area where his brother Bill had killed himself, after killing two men in the *Top House Tragedy*. Ethel thought this might have been the reason Ernest had moved away to North Island, away from the tittle tattle which had long followed the *murder suicide*.

Back in 1894, near the picturesque Alpine like village of St Arnaud, at the head of Nelson Lakes National Park, on the old boundary between Marlborough and Nelson, was the isolated *Top House* settlement. Ernest's brother Bill was a station hand, working the land around *Top House*, also tending the flocks of sheep. Six sheep had been first introduced into the country over a hundred years before in the 1770s by Capt. James Cook, though not very successfully, as four of the sheep he had taken aboard at the Cape of Good Hope never survived the journey, and the two which did, died shortly afterwards. having eaten poisonous plants. So, it wasn't until the 1850s that sheep farming became established and began to play an important role in the country's economy, and for decades wool from cross bred Merinos with long wool breeds, named Corriedale, accounted for nearly a third of New Zealand's exports by value.

The first flock of sheep, mainly Marino, was driven through the Nelson area in 1846 to the Wairau Valley and the first *Top House* hotel was a welcome stop on the journey from Nelson to the Wairau. In those days a meal, and chaff for the horse was four shillings. Then in 1887 a new cob hotel was built by a Nat Longney, planning to create a port of call for the sheep drovers working around the station. The natural building materials of clay, sand and straw mixed together ensured lots of beneficial properties. Thick walls, carrying heat late into the night during the colder months, then in summer keeping things cooler, and with a good roof of shingle shake - hand split wooden logs to compliment it, meant the cob could last for hundreds of years.

Nat Longney, like the Bateman family was also from Gloucester, England, and was married to Ernest and Bill's sister Louise. Ethel's sister-in-law for a short time. Bill in time had fallen for the housekeeper, a Miss Wiley at the *Top House*, writing letters to her in the hope she would go out with him. Regrettably she did not return his feelings. Eventually things came to a head when over-hearing in the hotel bar one evening some other local men laughing and joking about his unrequited love. He was so enraged with jealousy. An opportunity to pursue his love rival Colin Lane arose while his sister Louise and family were away in Blenheim. Planning to take him rabbit shooting the following afternoon, Bill borrowed a rifle from his friend William Wallis who worked at the Telegraph Station. Used to lending Bill his rifle for rabbit hunting William saw no problem this time either. Unknown to him, it was.

Arriving at the *Top House* the following afternoon, and after a dram of whisky and a chat, Bill persuaded Colin to join him for his usual rabbit hunt. The two men walked out into the paddock chatting away amiably. Bill, stopped to tie his boot lace. Then walking slowly behind Colin, who had continued on still talking and unaware, Bill raised his rifle, took aim and fired, shooting the hapless man in the back of the head. Moving over quickly to where Colin now lay, he dragged his lifeless body to the far side of the paddock, leaving it lying by the boundary fence.

Bill returned to the *Top House* and poured himself another whisky, pausing to ponder over what he had done. Realising that William would soon grasp it had been him who shot Colin Lane, as he had not long borrowed the rifle, friend or no friend, Bill had to act quickly. He went back to the Station and asked William to come with him as Colin had had an accident and needed help. Reaching Top House and running out to the paddock William saw Colin lying over at the far side by the fence. He made to cross the paddock, with Bill following behind, and once again taking aim, fired. He now had two bodies. Bill managed to cover both bodies with pieces of tarpaulin he found hanging nearby on the fence.

Returning to the *Top House* he cut the telegraph wires before drinking down several more whiskys. Unknown to him Miss Wiley the housekeeper had returned to the hotel finding no one there, yet there were several empty glasses and a half-finished bottle whisky, had the feeling that something was badly wrong. She ran as quickly as she could to the Telegraph Station and was surprised to find only Mrs Wallis, who was greatly concerned, as her husband had gone out with Bill a short time ago, but had not returned. Deciding to board themselves in as best they could for safety, Mrs Willis rang through an SOS to the Nelson Police. Shortly afterwards Bill turned up at the Telegraph Station but found the place boarded up and secure. Hardly able to breathe, the two ladies hiding under the counter, prayed that whoever was outside would go away. Bill realising a message must have been sent through to Nelson and to Blenheim, grasped fairly quickly what was going to happen, so made his way back to the

Hotel.

Later in the evening the eerie silence around *Top House* and the Telegraph Station was disturbed by the sound of a single gunshot.

Bill Bateman was found by the two constables who had arrived at the Station in answer to the earlier SOS call. On hearing the gun shot they ran to investigate. The disturbing scene they stumbled upon on the veranda of the hotel, was of Bateman lying barefoot and up against a post, the gun between his legs and a near empty bottle of whisky by his side. Somehow, he had managed to pull the trigger with his toe. The two other bodies were found the next morning in daylight. The full extent of the tragedy was then revealed.

After the Longney family returned to *Top House*, Bill's his sister Louise found a note addressed to her, telling her *not to weep for him and to give his love to his mother whom he would meet shortly in the next world, free from trouble and worry. Goodbye, Bill.*

The tragedy stirred up the community, and the Longney family eventually sold the business as no one wanted to visit or stay at the *Top House* anymore. Like Bill's brother Ernest, the family also moved to North Island, but to Palmerston North. Some sixty years after the catastrophe, in 1944 Nat Longney died at the age of ninety-six years. Nat and his family may have been long forgotten but the *Murder Suicide* memory at *Top House* lived on.

CHAPTER 8

West Coast Trip - South Island

1986

Hector stood listening for any further noise from the far end of the house, but all seemed quiet, apart from the blurred mixture of soft for a change, voices and country music from his stepson's room. No more sobbing came from their own bedroom, in fact no sound at all. He moved back to his seat at the table, glancing out of the window before sitting down. He had been hoping to be on the road by now, heading for Arthur's Pass hoping to reach the coast well before evening. Laying the letter back down on the table, he studied the envelope and stamp before picking the letter up again and holding both close. Breathing in slowly, but of course there was no scent, but just for a moment he felt close to who had carefully written his name and address in turquoise ink. He read the letter again, his first contact since the war with his long-lost daughter. How small she had been, how young he had been, in a world in turmoil, not knowing what the next day would bring. Incredibly it had brought two atom bombs, three days apart, detonated over Hiroshima and Nagasaki. The actions of the United States sent Hector back to the Pacific, so there had been little time to think of his daughter, as Japanese actions had first sent him there in 1942 to Guadalcanal, his memories flooded back.

Re reading the carefully worded letter, an enquiring letter, no nastiness, no meanness, just interest and caring. A lump formed in his throat as he folded it and put it back in the envelope. He left it on the table and he went back to continue packing the saloon. A sudden longing to be back down on the Paringa filled him. To be surrounded again by the sounds of the rainforest and the river, the fishing, the reassuring ebb and flow of the mighty Tasman Sea at the mouth of the river, and the ever-changing colours as the sun set out to the west. Every year they went down in September till November for the white baiting season, since the middle sixties when they had married, and this year would be no different, though there was every chance now it would be. The letter disappeared later that morning and it was many years before he came across it again.

Eventually with all their goods gathered and packed into the Honda, Hector had a last look round. Neil appeared from his old room saying he would lock up, also check on the house when he was up in town. He and his wife lived in a small holding south of the city. Having stables, a few horses, she gave riding lessons, while he concentrated on his sports coaching in the city, so checking on the house would be no inconvenience, also stay over, if need be, on a night out with friends. The young couple also enjoyed the odd weekend down the Paringa during the season, bringing mail and extra provisions as requested. Checking the house for mail would also give him a chance to keep an eye out for any further UK airmail letters.

Heading out west from Christchurch to Kirwee, Shefield and Springfield across the Canterbury plain to Arthur's Pass, on to Otira, turning off before Kumara to reach the coast at Hokitika, where they would happily bed down for the night at an old Returned Serviceman friend's house. Here they enjoyed his wife's homemade soup, and lamb stew, afterwards reminiscing over several beers before realising it was late and they had an early start. Leaving next morning soon after breakfast, after filling up with a flask of hot tea, some home baked lamingtons, which Cath put in a tin to be enjoyed later, they headed south along the west coast route 6. First to Ross, HariHari, then on to Franz Joseph Glacier, and Fox Glacier with the turn off to Gillespies Beach, before arriving at the bridge across the Paringa.

Here they would park their car and load up their things on Tom Connal the River Bailiff's jet boat, for the last stage of the journey to their wooden hand-built holiday home, where they would stay till mid-November, before heading back east. It was a good, simple life in the fresh air, and could be very profitable.

Settling in took time as they got older, but there was no rush. Cath was in charge indoors, and Hector outdoors, mostly. Not only were the fishing stands to be set up near the river mouth, as well as closer upstream, the small garden had to be tended after a winter of neglect, with a few new plantings, taken from cuttings of plants left untouched by the few cattle which roamed along the river bank in search of a tasty morsel. Rifles were checked, possums hunted and the quadbike serviced. While at times the season could be slow to start, the combination of increasing temperatures, spring tides and a little rain, created ideal conditions in September, October and November for lucrative white baiting. An early 5am start, till usually 8pm in the evening, made it a long day. Gathering the catch, packing it ready for collection by Tom to take speedily up to the bridge to be then transported by road to Greymouth, Nelson and Christchurch, or into Tom's freezers for later collection and delivery. This continued every day, along with the constant checking and mending of the fine meshed fishing nets, making it a fulltime, tiring job.

No mention of the airmail letter was raised during their stay down the river, and the season drifted on as usual. Neighbours came and went from other bachs close by, beers were enjoyed, drafts played and tales recalled from years gone by. Perhaps Cath seemed more withdrawn, only brightening up when her sister and brother-in-law came down the river for the odd weekend from Greymouth or her son came to stay for a few days. Walking by themselves and talking intently as they wandered along the river bank before reaching the sandy beach on the edge of the Tasman Sea. Hector was never privy to their conversations and it never bothered him, understanding their closeness from his days with Ethel. Both he and his step son at a young age having lost their fathers and growing up alone with their mothers, Hector understood the need to be alone together at times.

CHAPTER 9

Growing up – Nelson College

Mid 1930s

Ethel's and her son's nomadic life continued in and around the Dovedale and Nelson area. Sometimes living with family, sometimes in rented lodgings. Hector helped his mother manage to scrape a living helping out at fruit picking in autumn. Hop picking by hand was his first real job, and in summer, weeding and hoeing between the tobacco plants in the nearby farm, which surrounded their rented, wooden bungalow. It was tough work in the tobacco fields, under the warm sun, yet he began to earn more money as he got older. Tobacco had been grown in the Nelson and Blenheim area for many years, the soil being ideal pumice soil formed during volcanic eruptions. This part of the country sat atop the remains of an ancient volcanic plume and in 1914 ten people were killed by the debris flow. The volcanic soil enhances drainage which prevents the roots from rotting in any wet weather. Some farmers would give their sons an acre of land to grow tobacco plants, which they had to look after themselves, banking the money for their futures. Others grew potatoes or Huti Huti, kumara or sweet potatoes to sell, a pre-European species which had been used in Maori cuisine for centuries.

Hector as he grew older enjoyed helping around the farms, gaining experience as well working in the evenings at Motueka harbour, unloading the fishing boats of their catch of snapper, sea salmon, and blue cod. The fish were boxed and iced, prepared for the local markets, or sent on the overnight ferry from

Nelson to Wellington. By the age of twelve in 1936 conditions in Europe were deteriorating. In March of that year, Germany violated the Treaty of Versailles, reoccupying the Rhineland and the Spanish Civil War began with Francisco Franco named as Head of State. That same year Hector started at Nelson College, now structurally recovered from the 1929 earthquake. Ethel thought it best if he went to the boys' college with her other grandson Robert, from Nelson, being the same age. Hector would get a good education. adding to all he had learnt during his young years on the farm, then moving around the Golden Bay, Dovedale and Motueka areas, helping with all the seasonal work and as he grew older, down at the harbour too. All which she thought would stand him in good stead throughout his adult years.

Ethel, sad but proud seeing her adopted son growing up so quickly, knew she would miss him, yet pleased that he seemed ready to go away to school. She started gathering his things together, finally making him promise to write to her, regularly. Going with Hector on the bus to Nelson to meet Colin and half-brother Robert again, as Colin had offered to then take them to the College, see the boys settled before taking Ethel back home. Another chapter of Hector's life was beginning, and Ethel would be on her own the first time since she moved away from Taranaki to have her baby Eva back in 1889.

Nelson College for Boys was founded in 1856, the motto *Loyalty, Honesty and Wisdom*. In 1870 the college took part in the first game of Rugby in New Zealand against the Nelson Rugby Football Club.

Hector and Robert were boarders, though the school also had day boys. It was a strict regime; the caning era ran from the start in 1856 for over a hundred years. New boys were initiated into a school tradition in the gym to test their fortitude, by running the gauntlet passed the older boys armed with wet knotted towels, lashing out at the new, younger boys as they ran past. Pretty daunting for the young boys, and for many, worse was to come.

Average in academic studies, Hector with his good hand and eye co-ordination developed guddling for fish and hand-picking fruit deftly, excelled on the playing fields, at cricket and tennis, advancing to county level as he grew older. Many years later during the war, he played for the Royal Navy team at Lords cricket ground in London. He wrote regularly to Ethel as promised, which delighted her. Never mentioning anything about the caning, concentrating instead on his enjoyment of cricket and tennis, and that he was now a member of the Radio club and was learning to work in wireless and telephony. Ethel enjoyed writing to him too, keeping him up to date with news of Roddie, who was missing him, and recalling all the fun they had teasing the old minister.

Another of the unwritten rules Hector never mentioned was, that Juniors were only allowed cold showers, summer and winter. Late one afternoon the younger boys, tired, sore, wet and cold after playing a game of rugby on the playing field in front of the college, were heading back in to the changing rooms to shower and change. One of their team lingering behind after their showers, deciding after the other boys had gone through to the changing rooms, to take the chance of a hot shower as he was so cold and sore. Hardly having the chance to relish the treat, the boy was suddenly and roughly dragged out of the shower by an older prefect, who turning the tap to cold shoved him back under. The boy turning on the prefect hit him as hard as he could. Retaliating with callousness, the older boy dragged the naked, shouting, wet junior out of the shower block over to the Housemaster's room. After explaining what had happened, the Housemaster dealt the most severe flogging, oblivious of the boy's pleas to stop. Following this, the older boy pushing the now sobbing junior along to the prefects' study, chalked marks on the floor around the boy's feet where he was standing. Making him bend over to touch his toes, the head prefect then climbed onto a footstool gaining some extra height and leverage before bringing the cane down with resounding blows. The pain, so excruciating, the boy practically flew out of the room, his feet hardly touching the floor. The other boys hearing the shouting, witnessed this barbaric treatment but from a safe distance, understood; the rule for cold showers, which continued for the rest of their stay at the college and was never abused again.

Life was indeed hard, a world away from Dovedale and his mother. Ethel occasionally as promised, kept Dolly, now married and living on the West Coast at Coal Creek Flats, informed of her son's progress. Then in 1938 as it seemed the rest of the world was on the move, Dolly too would soon be on the move, from the west coast back to Christchurch, but not of her own freewill. This time alone with her ten-year-old son Sid and five-year-old daughter Virginia, and ten shillings in her pocket, she set off to try to start a new life.

CHAPTER 10

HMS/HMNZS Philomel

1890 - 1949

New Zealand in contrast to its entry into the First World War, acted in its own right by formally declaring war on Nazi Germany alongside Great Britain on 3rd September 1939, following Germany's invasion of Poland on the 1st September, in accordance with the expiry of the British government's ultimatum to Germany to withdraw from Poland.

New Zealand forces were soon serving across Europe. The forces were known for their strength and determination in Northern Africa and Southern Europe, even the German Commander Rommel was known to have said 'Give me the Māori Battalion and I will conquer the world.'

Prior to the outbreak of the First World War the New Zealand Government had been trying to establish its own naval forces to compliment the forces of the Australian Navy. Persuading the British government to provide New Zealand with a cruiser, the Royal Navy offered the aging and outdated Pearl-class cruiser *HMS Philomel*, which would however revert to the Royal Navy in time of war. The *Philomel* launched in Devonport, England in1890, already had had an eventful 24-year career before it was commissioned to New Zealand in 1914.

As Europe stumbled towards war in July 1914, New Zealand commissioned the *Philomel* as its first warship. Then in the August it reverted to the Royal navy with the New Zealand government continuing to pay the crew's wages and maintenance of the ship throughout the war. The first task in late August 1914 was to escort the Advance Party of the New Zealand Expeditionary Force to German Samoa, with Hector's father James part of the crew. Some twenty-five years later Hector in 1939 joined the *Philomel's* training function as a telegraphist, straight from Nelson College.

During the interwar period the ship's superstructure had been removed to make room for classroom training space, huts to accommodate the naval cadets and officers, and recommissioning as a Training Base. Steaming from her base at Wellington across the Cook Strait out into the Tasman Sea in the northwest, and continuing north to the dockyard at the Auckland Naval base. It was here the *Philomel* housed the volunteers from 1939 to 1941. Commissioned again in 1941 till 1945 when the old ship was eventually sold for scrap. At sunset on the 16th of January 1946 the Navy's White Ensign was ceremoniously lowered for the last time. However it wasn't until three years later in August 1949 with a fitting ritualistic end in the sea a few miles from a small uninhabited island, Cuvier Island, off the east coast of North Island, the hulk of the 90-year-old ship loaded with 4kg of explosives was sent to its watery Pacific grave.

CHAPTER 11

No Luck - No Gold

1998

In spite of the cold and pain, Hector managed to scramble to his feet and regain his balance, before leaning back against a centuries old tree fern, whose luxuriance, dominance and appeal, ensured its position as the main symbol of the country. He gazed up through the silver-white under surface of the mature fronds to the soft grey evening sky, and drawing some strength he hoped, from this ancient fern, managed to get his baring as the light began to fade. He knew he hadn't walked far before he being shot at, therefore his tent wasn't too far beneath the point where he had fallen. Maybe the joker had been hunting possum, not uncommon in this area, but he felt he would have spotted or heard him, whereas the prone figure, caught him unawares, and unable to defend himself. He was older and slower now, but he still knew his way about the bush and rain forest, recalling life in his deer culling days back in the late fifties, early sixties.

Moving slowly, he managed to retrace his steps over the rough forest floor, stopping occasionally to catch his breath and support his left arm which he held across his chest as if in an imaginary sling. Reaching the edge of the slope above where his tent was pitched, he managed carefully to lower himself using his good arm, and edging himself as best he could down the rough gradient till he reached the stoney path leading to his tent. Everything seemed as it was when he had left earlier. Easing himself inside and on to his sleeping bag he sat till his breathing was back to normal and his mind had stopped racing, then he managed to rummaged through in his rucksack. He found his torch, a flask of water, several handkerchiefs and a bag of sphagnum moss. After managing to open the flask by balancing it between his knees, he took a drink of water, he eased his injured arm slowly out of his anorak and managed to rip his shirt sleeve exposing the wound. He succeeded without spilling any water to soak one of the handkerchiefs and clean the exposed flesh as best he could, then covered the wound with some of the sphagnum moss, before wrapping his arm with the torn sleeve to hold the moss in place. Knowing sphagnum moss absorbs liquid, staunches any blood and eventually helps the wound to heal, he felt he had done the best he could in the circumstances. Hector then ate a few of the biscuits he had left and sipped some more water, by then he was pretty bushed. Lying down and making himself as comfortable as he could, he hoped to manage a few hours' sleep, even if fitful.

The helicopter pilot Scott Norris had said when dropping Hector off, he would return for him in four days. Remembering this, Hector knew he had time to rest, and time to clear up his makeshift camp before heading out to Gillespies Beach. Gillespies was a stunning long, black sand beach with tons of shells and pebbles, bounded by Westland Tai Poutini National Park and the Tasman Sea.

Hector started going over in his mind everything that had happened. He couldn't work out who else knew he was down the coast, not at his bach as would have been expected, but prospecting in the bush for some long-lost small gold seam. Never mentioning to anyone over the years that he and his friend Allan Rodgers had stumbled across the small seam many years before, back in the nineteen fifties, always planning they would come back someday and claim their find. Tragically Allan had been killed in an air crash down the South Westland. The Tiger Moth aircraft's motor began to splutter over dense bush only two miles after take-off. The pilot managed to turn the plane round and was heading back when the motor cut out, crashing, with the loss of both lives. So sadly the friends never made it back to find the gold as they had planned.

Hector finally marrying a few years later, a widow Cath Lewis from a west coast farming family, with a young son Neil. She had died recently, unexpectedly, never having resolved their argument over the airmail letter from the United Kingdom, especially the fact that Hector had a grown-up daughter and had never told her. Tidying out her wardrobe in the family home in Christchurch shortly after her death, he unexpectedly came across the long-lost airmail letter. Hidden at the back of the wardrobe underneath a tartan rug funnily enough, was an old shoe box, and this is where Cath had hidden it. The cause of so much bother over the years was now back in his hands, and now here he was sitting in his tent, injured, having been shot at, maybe accidentally, maybe not, as the culprit had run off leaving Hector where he fell. Then the mystery of hearing a helicopter fly over and on up the Paringa. This was his first time down the river since Cath's death and funeral in Westlands, in fact not far from where he now was. Being on his own at home in Christchurch was no bother, as he had felt he had needed the break away from his wife's family. Away from people in general, with time to think, and down the Paringa was the answer, yet everything was happening so quickly, that he didn't feel in control, not a good feeling.

Having an address and number after all this time, although realising both may have changed. However, as luck would have it, and after a bit of research he eventually made telephone contact with a couple who knew where his daughter and family now lived. After the initial unbelievable contact, they continued phoning and writing, faxing too, with both keen and excited to meet after all these years. Deciding she would fly to Christchurch; plans were going ahead to meet in a couple of months' time, in the autumn. He felt like a young man again. Perhaps the feeling of having regained some type of contact with his only love Lizzie after all these years, a lifetime really, through his daughter, he could hardly believe it.

Life was beginning to feel good again and it was. Then he remembered the gold. The plans he and Allan had had, and somehow now seemed as good a time as any, so he started planning his trip to the coast. He was so sure as he drifted off to sleep, he would be able to find the spot even after all these years, confident too that Allan would guide him.

CHAPTER 12

Off to War

1941

In 1940, at sixteen, Hector left Nelson College a wiser, stronger and fitter young man. Having studied and qualified in Radio Technology, and like several of his fellow students, decided to join the services, and continue his training in the RNZN on *HMS Philomel.* In April that year, Germany invaded Norway and occupied Denmark, the war had begun in earnest. A month later German forces swept through Belgium and the Netherlands, in the *lightning war*, or *Blitzkrieg.*

Prior to starting his naval training Hector managed to spend a few days with Ethel in the rented farm cottage near Motueka, lending a hand with fruit picking, and tidying up the yard as autumn was settling in. His cousin Roddie, eighteen months younger, was excited to hear about Hector's move to join the navy, also pleased to be able to spend some time with him before he set off. They had been great friends as young boys, full of fun and mischief. So, wanting to enlist for war service too, Roddie, like many young men, was planning to give false details about his age, and was eager to hear what Hector had to say. His mother Mavis however, suspicious of Roddie's ideas after Hector left, told him he had to put such notions out of his head, he was needed at home for a while yet, she still needed him to help on the small holding.

Life was certainly changing.

As in World War One, the fighting seemed to be thousands of

miles away in Europe, until a surprise military strike by the Imperial Japanese Navy Air Service early on Sunday morning 8th December 1941, upon the United States base at Pearl Harbour in Honolulu, Hawaii. The attack was intended to prevent the United States Pacific Fleet from interfering with Japanese military actions in Southeast Asia against the United Kingdom's and the Netherland's overseas territories. The next day the United States, a neutral country until then, formally entered the war.

Before departing for active service on the *HMNZS Achilles*, Hector had leave to visit Ethel in Motueka. As this would be his last visit home for several years, Ethel gave him his birth mother Dolly's address in Christchurch, asking him to visit her on his way to the Banks Peninsula, feeling it would be important for both of them to meet before he went off to war. Hector organised himself, visiting family, paying farewell visits to friends and enjoying a few beers with the fisherman

, before travelling by bus from Nelson down the east coast via Kaikoura to Christchurch. He was meeting up with his ship at Littleton Harbour on the peninsula, so Christchurch fortunately was on his way.

Following the outbreak of war in 1939 and New Zealand's declaration of war, there were many changes to everyday life. Petrol rationing, and shortage of materials such as rubber, affecting the use of private motorcars, hence prompting a boost to public transport. There were also large numbers of military personnel stationed in and around the city. The Army at Burnham Camp, the Airforce at Wigram Aerodrome, and a contingent of American soldiers based in Christchurch too.

Wanting to please Ethel and partly out of curiosity, he found his way to Durham Street, after arriving at Cathedral Square, already bustling with both civilians and military. Meeting his mother for the first time since 1924, when she had handed him over in Nelson to *the kind lady*, was certainly something he had never imagined, or ever really thought about, until now. Knocking on the door of the small apartment above the baker's shop he listened, he knocked again, then heard a woman's voice calling him to come away in. Closing the door behind him he went along the narrow hallway and called out, 'Hello, Hector here'.

The reply came from the room on the right at the end of the narrow hall. The door opened into a living room, where he found Dolly resting against the pillows on her bed, in the bed recess. Feeling awkward and wondering if she was ill, he managed to stumble out the words that Ethel had given him the address, asking him to come and see her as he was going off to war. Dolly gazed at him, unable to say anything, unable to believe this could really be her long-lost son. She continued looking at the young sailor, then asked him to sit down on the edge of the bed till she got a better look at him.

Here he was, Hector, a young man now, the baby she had given away all those years ago, so difficult to take the situation in. Going off to war with every chance he would not return. What could she say in such a short time. All she was able to do was stretch out and touch his hand, then withdrew it quickly. Hector said nothing, but smiled, looking at the attractive, dark-wavy haired stranger, searching her face. What do you say? Who are you? Who am I? All too much, and life at this time was so uncertain. At that moment he heard the noise of feet running up the stairs, the door opened and in came a pretty, dark-haired young girl of about eight. Flinging her school bag down on the bed and saying as she stared at Hector,

'Who is this Mummy?'

Hector rose from the bed, tentatively squeezing Dolly's still outstretched hand, before walking to the door, glancing round, he smiled at his mother and his young half-sister. Saying to himself under his breath,

'Goodbye mother, at least we did meet again'.

'That's your big brother Hector, Virginia, he is going off to war,' Dolly answered, her throat tightening and tears filling her eyes.

Virginia smiled saying nothing, instead skipped over to the sink to pour herself a drink of water and one for her mother. Then sitting up on the bed beside her she started chatting about her day at school. The games she had played with her friends in the playground and the homework she had to do. With that she jumped down off the bed, opened her school bag pulled out a jotter and pencil, some coloured crayons and went over and sat at the table. All thoughts of the young sailor soon gone. It wasn't the first time she had met a young sailor on the stairs as she came home, but at least this sailor had smiled warmly at her. Unbeknown to young Virginia she would be nearly sixty-six years old before they met again.

Watching her daughter settle happily with her homework, Dolly lay down, turning towards the wall and burying her head in the pillow to stifle the sobs. The pain of giving her son away returning, twisting inside, even after all this time. Repeating over and over to herself, how do you tell your son why you had to give him away, while keeping your other son. How do you explain that? Was he not really wanted? No, I guess he wasn't at the time. She was lonely and someone cared, just the wrong someone. All too complicated, and here she was on her own again, with a young daughter who needed her, this was important now. Hector had grown into a fit young man, off to war, you certainly don't say anything at a surprise first meeting, nor at this time in his life, maybe never, you keep it to yourself, as she had always done. Dolly fell asleep with Virginia now curled up beside her, homework finished, trying to ignore the niggling hunger twinges in her tummy as it neared their meal time. Somehow, she knew her mother needed her close, though too young to fully understand, and she needed her mother as all little girls do. So, cuddling even closer and feeling safe, dinner could wait.

Walking smartly and quickly hoping to clear his head, Hector made his way back to Cathedral Square to continue his journey to Lyttleton. The buses were frequent and busy, the journey to Norwich Quay around thirty minutes or so. He was pleased, he couldn't have faced a long laborious journey with all the mixed-up thoughts and feelings swirling around in his head. Not just meeting his birth mother for the first time, now a young sister too, also saying goodbye to Ethel, not knowing if he would ever see her again, that was hard.

More disturbing however was what he was about to face, as he set out to fight for King and Country, though he knew he was well trained and understood duty unquestionably came first. All other things in his mind regarding today would soon fall into place. Though certainly not into the place he was now heading.

CHAPTER 13

HMS Achilles - Pacific

1942-1943

The United States Marine Corps' amphibious base was on the Province of the Solomon Islands at Guadalcanal, and it was here that *HMNZS Achilles* on convoy duty was where Hector would experience his first military campaign.

Hector's family now, was the crew of the Leander-class light cruiser *HMNZS Achilles,* built by Cammel Laird & Company Birkenhead, England, launched in 1932 and commissioned into the Royal navy in 1933.

The young sailors and officers were together twenty-four hours a day out in the South Pacific Ocean, sailing between the United States vessels, changing course at short notice to avoid attacks from Japanese ships and aircraft, and nearly colliding into each other more often than not. The crew worked three hourly shifts so never managing a full night's sleep. The training certainly mentally prepared them for the worst. Constant torpedo and air attacks, with many near misses, till the Japanese with fanatical bombardment eventually managed to bomb the *Achilles.* Blowing the top off the X turret, killing thirteen of the crew, including the young sailor working alongside Hector.

Along with the rest of the crew Hector said a final farewell to his friend, who with the other less fortunate young sailors, lay wrapped in their weighted hammocks under their respective flags, then at the poignant sound of the bugle, their bodies were lowered into the Pacific to rest forever in an unknown watery grave.

After the attack the *Achilles* was directed on to Portsmouth, England, to be 'patched up', taking onboard at the request of the Americans, rescued seaman from a seriously damaged Russian merchant ship. The Russian merchant marines who, practically ate the *Achilles* crew out of food rations and supplies by the time they reached England, were more than happy to have been rescued. Not only had they survived and now sailing to a safer haven, but were at last well fed.

Arriving safely at Portsmouth, the great first naval port of the United Kingdom, on the Solent, South Hampshire, the *Achilles* was manoeuvred into dry dock for repairs. During this time the German Luftwaffe bombed the United Kingdom's only waterfront city, Portsmouth, hoping to bomb the ship that had been one of the three ships at the demise of the *Graf Spee* during the Battle of the River Plate in 1939, the first naval battle of the war. Luckily the *Achilles* escaped this air mounted attack, unlike the unfortunate people of Portsmouth.

Some three months later as the crew were preparing to return to their ship disaster struck, there was an explosion aboard the vessel caused by a gas torch being left on by one of the welders. The crew consequently ended up staying in England longer than planned, with the *Achilles* eventually returning to the Pacific, being stationed off Okinawa till the end of the war with Japan in August 1945.

Hector, like others from the *Achilles* was transferred to the Royal Navy, this time as a telegraphist on Royal Navy submarines. He was soon sailing out of the English Channel into the Irish Sea heading north, his first sighting of Scotland being the long-extinct volcano, Ailsa Craig, in the outer Firth of Clyde. Sailing on, in some of the deepest waters in Europe, between the Scottish mainland and the majestic Isle of Arran, along the sheltered east coast of the compact Island of Bute, reaching his destination. Lush and fertile, with rolling hills, craggy heather covered moorlands on the north of the island and sandy beaches around the coastline, the submarine sailed round Craigmore headland on into Rothesay Bay. It would be here in this far off north west corner of war-torn Europe, that Hector's life would change forever.

CHAPTER 14

Gillespies Beach - Uplift

1998

Around 1865 a prospector, Gillespie, discovered gold here and soon a bustling settlement grew of around several hundred people, though by the 1920s the settlement was a ghost town, their names remembered only by a historic cemetery hidden amongst the bracken, a reminder of the hardy miners who lost their lives seeking gold. Reviving for a short time in the nineteen thirties and forties, the lure of gold always tempting, as Hector knew only too well.

Sunrise, Hector's favourite time of day filtered in through the tent, time to be getting up and getting on. The lingering pain in his upper arm reminding him it wasn't going to be easy. Trying to lift himself up from his makeshift bed every part of his body seemed to be aching. He reached out for his flask and sipped some less than fresh water, but none the less welcoming as it slipped over his dry throat. Easing back against his rucksack and gathering his thoughts he looked at his watch. Realising what he had to do and the state he was in, he had better start to make a move, no matter how slowly or how painful. Deciding the basics was all he could manage to take with him; considering the several miles of rough terrain he had to cross and the fact he was in his seventies, and injured.

Realising it hadn't been a wise situation to find himself in, in fact as it had turned out, a very unwise situation. Yet the mix up of recent emotions had propelled him on to try to achieve what in reality was impossible. However, the truth being, he had to somehow manage to negotiate the very rocky, slippery at times, rain forest floor, to get himself to the only possible landing place along at Gillespies Beach. Many times, over the years he had been on Gillespies Beach, a favoured spot for campers and hikers out to experience the wildness and impressive views of pebbled beaches and jagged coastlines along the edge of the Tasman Sea. The snow-covered towering peaks of Mount Cook and the Southern Alps a spectacular backdrop to this magnificent isolated part of the world.

His arm throbbed as he started moving, gathering his things together. Knowing he needed proper medical attention; it was fortunate that the medical centre was reasonably close by the heliport. Beginning to bother him about as much as the pain, was explaining how it had happened, without inviting too many questions from the nursing staff. Leaving his tent folded as best he could and hidden out of the way, he picked up his roughly hewn walking stick before manoeuvring his rucksack on to his good shoulder. Picking his way along the forest floor, attentive eyes high in the branches followed his every step with the sound of the dawn chorus filling the air.

Continuing to make his way down out of the rain forest, into the bush before eventually reaching the pebbly beach, where he could see lying among the driftwood, and oblivious to gold, a furry seal colony, keeping a vigilant eye on wandering sightseers, who had a habit of getting between them and their escape, the sea. Hector kept his eye on the seals as he made his way to the campsite and car park. Thankfully he sat on a tussock for a well-earned rest, his rucksack and stick by his side, patiently waiting. He had a few biscuits and some cheese left in his bag which he finished, washing it down with what was left of the water in his flask. His three flasks now empty.

After about half an hour he heard a chopper's engine which he hoped was heading his way this time. Scott Lewis, skilfully brought the small red Robinson chopper in to land, watched by a relieved Hector and also now by a small gathering of curious tourists. As the down draft eased and the blades came to rest, the awaiting passenger acknowledged Scott's wave. Picking up his few bits and pieces, he made his way over the stoney car park, to the small two-seater chopper, helped this time by one of the curious onlookers. With Scott's and the young hiker's help Hector managed up into the chopper. After sitting down, he lent over and handed his young helper the hewn stick.

'Keep it, you may need it someday, thanks for your help.'

Scott checked the passenger door was securely shut, after helping Hector to belt up, then going round got himself back in and belted up too. Checking the instruments prior to starting up the engine, the red chopper soon lifted into the air. The small crowd of onlookers moved well back out of the way, waving and shouting to the duo as they swept round and out towards the sea before heading along the coast north over Fox Glacier and on to Hokitika. The group chatted for a few minutes watching the helicopter eventually disappear from sight before they split up and continued on their separate ways along the coast of this remote part of South Island. The little bit of excitement over, but something to recall at some later date. Unaware of the story behind it all or of what was yet to come.

'So, no gold then Hector?' Scott stated, rather than questioned, 'not this time anyway, pity about that, you were so sure, and seems you have injured yourself as well, what happened? But hey, what's this about the emergency on Paringa beach a couple of days ago? I wasn't on call but heard when I came in the following day, yesterday in fact. Pretty bad in seems from all accounts. Happened near your old bach it turns out, no doubt the Greymouth police will be in touch with you. You might even need to go back down and check the property, a quad bike was involved, I believe.'

Remaining quiet, Hector struggled to make out all Scott was

saying, over the noise of the engine and blades. Better to say nothing, hey, he didn't know anyway. He kept looking ahead, the only memory he had, being of the helicopter flying over as he lay injured, and thinking it was coming for him. His mind was again whirling like the blades, too much of a coincidence not to have something to do with the shooting, but best say nothing. He would learn sooner rather than later, though his gut feeling was, better later.

The flight was quick and uneventful thankfully, remembering his friend Alan's tragic end on his return flight years ago, during one of their white baiting seasons. Touching down they were met by Caitlin Hughes, married to a second cousin of his late wife. Caitlin helped out at the helicopter station and quickly realising Hector had a problem, decided to take him over to the Medical Centre and have him checked over. Walking over to her car she suggested to Hector that he could stay over at their house, have a hot meal and a bed for the night. She realised there was a problem for Hector to drive home now, so perhaps her husband Rhys could take him back east the following day in Hector's own Honda, which was parked at the small airport. Rhys had to drive over to pick up a Toyota Hilux truck in Christchurch, and would have needed a lift from someone anyway. This would suit both, sort of two birds with one stone. Hector agreed, relieved, and thanked her. Freshening up as best he could, Caitlin, having phoned ahead, took him over to the Centre, with Hector hoping not too many questions would be asked.

Taking Hector into the curtained off examination bay, the triage nurse looked at his arm, commenting on his homemade dressing of sphagnum moss. Saying he had done well; however, she would need to numb the area before she thoroughly inspected it, and pressure cleaned before suturing the wound. Asking how it happened, he mumbled about tripping over while possum hunting, his rifle going off, falling over, and hitting his head before passing out. Couldn't remember much when he came too, but did recall he had some moss in his bag. A useful tip from his deer culling days in the Alps.

'Well, you were lucky,' she pointed out, 'no serious damage, a flesh wound, we will soon tidy that up. Oh, and by the way where is your rifle now?' Caught off guard, he paused before saying that when he came to, he knew he had to tend to his wound so must have left it where it fell. Then forgot about it in his fluster to get ready in time for his chopper ride back.

'OK, so you know nothing of the dreadful accident down the Paringa then, the quad bike accident. We heard the 'joker' has been taken on to Christchurch after being flown direct to Greymouth. Not sure they are even capable of dealing with his injuries in Christchurch. Reckon he will never walk again. Very sad. Foolish, driving so fast on the pebbly beach as if the devil himself was after him I heard, before hitting a beached tree. Wouldn't know a thing till the air ambulance arrived.'

By the time the nurse had finished her account, his wound was cleaned, stitched and bandaged and she was about to put his arm in a sling.

'Someone coming for you?' she asked, 'best have some help for a few days.'

With that Cait popped her head round the curtain.

'Good,' said the nurse, 'you take care, you are not getting any younger. Maybe leave possum hunting to the younger jokers in future.'

Still feeling a bit achy, though a lot better since his pain relief and treatment, Cait and Hector set off for the car park, chatting about what they should have for dinner. Hector visualising a cold beer, and hopefully a good nights sleep.

The nurse chatting away ten to the dozen had saved him trying to answering any more awkward questions, but deep down he had the feeling the answers to the recent drama were not what he wanted to hear.

CHAPTER 15

Isle of Bute - Scotland

Chance Meeting

1943

Strategically placed on higher ground overlooking Rothesay Bay is the unusual circular Rothesay Castle, complete with moat. Originally built as a defence against the Norwegian Realm back at the beginning of the 13th century, it had close links with the Crichtons who were hereditary High Stewards of Scotland, and then from 1371 the Royal dynasty.

Rothesay, on the Isle of Bute, developed into a seaside resort on the Firth of Clyde from the Victorian era well on into the twentieth century. Though small in size the Island played a crucial part in Britain's war effort. Within hours of Prime Minister Neville Chamberlain's announcement that Britain was now at war with Germany, Bute's response to the declaration was immediate.

War had been looming over Europe for months, and Glasgow, like all big cities in Britain, made contingency plans for moving children away from the dangers of assumed German air raids. Within hours of the announcement eight hundred and sixty children along with teachers and helpers, arrived in Rothesay on the paddle steamer *Jeanie Deans*, followed later that day by another six hundred and fifty children again aboard the *Jeanie Deans*. By the following day another one thousand six hundred children landed at Rothesay Pier off two other Clyde Steamers. Many of the steamers went on to serve as mine sweepers, even taking part in the evacuation of Dunkirk between 26th May and 4th June 1940. A few also serving as troopships, others as accommodation vessels moored on the Clyde serving the Boom Defence depot.

Upon arrival in early September 1939, the young evacuees were taken to the Rothesay Pavilion and provided with hastily prepared food, then later billeted in private homes. This was an official decree and anyone with a spare room had to comply. Householders were paid ten shillings and sixpence per week for one child, and eight shillings and sixpence per child if more than one child was billeted.

As well as evacuees, the island was immediately mobilised with all the relevant services and agencies, so Bute's World War covered all spectrums of military activity. Due to the island's secluded and insular situation in the Clyde estuary, Naval involvement was predominant. HMS Cyclops 7th Submarine Flotilla was the home base in Rothesay. Launched in October 1905 in Sunderland, serving in the Great War as a depot ship in the Mediterranean, HMS Cyclops was finally scrapped in 1947 near Newport, Wales, on the River Usk close to its confluence with the Severn Estuary.

A few miles north along the coast from Rothesay at Port Bannatyne was the Royal Navy shore establishment, the base for Operation Source. The Head Quarters for the 12th Submarine Flotilla, was HMS Varbel, the requisitioned 88 roomed Kyles Hydro Hotel, overlooking the Port. This was the only British base for midget submarines and human torpedo training. The secure waters of Loch Striven north of the Port were used for sea trials and training, including beach reconnaissance and navigation. It was here too that the heroic, daring raid on the German battleship Tirpitz was masterminded and later executed. This was now the world in which Hector found himself, with autumn in Argyll slowly drawing in.

> The lazy mist hangs from the brow of the hill,
>
> Concealing the course of the dark winding rill;
>
> How languid the scenes, late so sprightly appear,
>
> As autumn to winter resigns the pale year.

>   Robert Burns (1759-1796)

HMS Cyclops built by Laing & Son, Sunderland, for the Indra Line Ltd., then bought by the Admiralty prior to launching in October in 1905, and commissioned two years later. A Royal Naval submarine repair and depot ship, the mother ship, was berthed in Rothesay Bay in the Clyde estuary, near the mouth of Loch Striven and surrounded by the Argyllshire hills. Hector was reminded of the equally beautiful setting around the Banks peninsular, where he had set sail for war in 1942 on HMNZS Achilles. Lake Forsyth and the French settlement of Akaroa, on South Island, south east of Christchurch, now with spring approaching, thousands of miles away, was still clear in his mind, as was his mother Ethel.

Rowing over from the mother ship to Rothesay pier, the young sailors enjoyed their time ashore. Eating and drinking in the various local pubs and tearooms along Victoria Street, or wandering along the promenade with the spectacular views out across the bay to Toward lighthouse on the Argyll peninsular on the Scottish mainland, and further eastward over the Clyde to the Ayrshire coast. In Montague Street, the main shopping street below the castle and one street behind Victoria Street was the Victoria tearoom where one afternoon Lizzie caught Hector's eye.

Lizzie petite, with a mass of dark wavy hair and a quick ready smile, caught the eye of many of the lads who were as keen to chat to her, while serving the tables, as she was with them.

Tripping back and forth to the kitchen bringing an endless supply of tea, homemade scones and fairy cakes for the hungry lads, she knew her mother who owned the restaurant would be pleased. Later on, one afternoon as the group from Cyclops were paying and chatting to the owner at the till on their way out, Hector hung back, waiting on Lizzie reappearing from the kitchen. The dark wooden panelled door swung back and forth as she came out onto the shop floor again smiling, awkwardly he introduced himself. Lizzie catching his different accent asked where he was from, she was intrigued, never having met anyone from so far away before.

'New Zealand,' she whispered, 'I have never met anyone from there before.'

'Oh yeah?' he replied, 'You would like it. Not so different from what I have seen of Bute so far, very like South Island where I come from. Mountains, rolling hills, farmland, fishing and lovely beaches, perhaps the weather is a bit warmer in summer and less cold in winter, though the high tops are snow covered most of the year. Our west coast has very heavy rain off and on all year, a bit like Scotland as I am learning.' Hector described, laughing.

Realising the others had left the tearoom, Hector knew he would have to go. Quickly agreeing to meet up another afternoon, she watched him run back along the street to the square which led down to the pier. Dreamily she turned back into the shop as Hector ran to catch up with his shipmates who were whistling and making kissing sounds at him as he approached. He was laughing but undeniably felt a spring in his step, had a smile on his face and for the first time in his life, suddenly felt life wasn't so bad after all.

CHAPTER 16

Scapa Flow

1944/45

As autumn days were cooling and shortening with winter approaching, the war entered its fifth year. Their blossoming relationship found Hector and Lizzie spending as much time together as possible. Having her own small two room flat in Bridge Street, Lizzie gave Hector a spare key. However, more often than not he was away on duty, submerged under the waters off the west coast of Scotland, separated by the archipelago of the Inner Hebrides. Islay, Mull and Skye being the three largest of the 34 inhabited islands and 44 uninhabited islands. Out into The Minch, the colloquial name used by foreign sailors and fishermen, previously known as La Manche, supposedly populated by mythical creatures, storm kelpies or the blue men of the Minch looking out for boats to sink and sailors to drown. The strait or sea channel separated the north west Highlands of Scotland from the northern Inner Hebrides, and the Outer Hebrides of Lewis and Harris, and flowing on out into the treacherous eight-mile Pentland Firth. Rather a Strait than a Firth, separating the Orkney Islands from Caithness in the north of the Scottish mainland. A dangerous area for all sailing craft, between Duncansby Head and South Ronaldsay with the tidal flows reaching twelve knots and creating tidal swell waves of several metres high. This is where the Atlantic Ocean meets the North Sea.

The main naval base for the British Home Fleet during World War 1 and WorldWar 11 lay in Scapa Flow, and where Hector was now heading in his submarine. Back in 14th October 1939, a month in to the war, the Revenge-class battleship *Royal Oak* anchored in Scapa Flow, Orkney, was torpedoed by the German submarine U-47. The first torpedo was launched around 1.04am then several more torpedoes, till at 1.29am *Royal Oak* rolled to starboard and sank.

Of *Royal Oak's* complement of 1,234 men and boys, 835 were killed that night, many dying later of their wounds. This was one of Britain's worst naval disasters, more so because it happened in the middle of the famous and supposedly impregnable naval base. U-47 was then able to pass undetected back through Kirk Sound and return to Wilhelmshaven to be met by Grand Admiral Raeder and Admiral Donitz, who were later flown to Berlin for an audience with the Fuhrer. This bonanza for the Nazis was a public relations nightmare for the Admiralty, with resulting propaganda and recriminations.

On 21st May 1941 *HMS Hood* had weighed anchor around midnight sailing out of Scapa Flow through Hoxa Sound to patrol the waters south of Iceland on the summer route to the Arctic Ocean, the intention to prevent Germany's largest battleship *Bismarck* from reaching the North Atlantic. Three days later the unimaginable happened, *Bismarck* sank the pride of the British fleet at the *Battle of Denmark Strait*, between Iceland and Greenland. A bombardment from *Bismarck* hit *Hood*, there was an enormous explosion and the ship broke in half, sinking within minutes. With a crew of 1,419 only three survived. Three days later in the North Atlantic off the west coast of France, *Bismarck* was finally destroyed by two torpedoes fired from *HMS Dorsetshire*. After withstanding two hours of bombardment, Admiral Lutjens went down with his ship, along with 2,089 others.

Returning safely to Rothesay and to the arms of his lovely Lizzie, who was full of questions, he recalled that the waters of Scapa Flow were very cold indeed.

'How did you know that?' Lizzie quizzed.

'Well, I was in swimming,'

'Swimming! Swimming! It's a wonder you didn't freeze to death or drown.'

'Egged on, wasn't I, by the rest of the jokers. I volunteered to swim out to retrieve our football. They flung me a life buoy eventually, but only because it was the only football we had, well that's how the story goes.'

'Oh, so you weren't really fighting in the war then? And I've been so worried. Worried every day you were away, not knowing what was happening, not knowing how you were, where you were, or if you were even still alive.'

She flung the damp dishcloth at him, missing.

'Just as well you weren't there then, with your aim.'

He came over and wrapped his arms round her, feeling her warmth and deep feelings stirring within himself. They left the dishes, following their instincts instead. Much later, both happy to be together again and basking in the now quiet and loving peace of their long-awaited union, slept till morning. Unbeknown to them, in the shadowy mystery of life, two became three.

Again, Hector's life was about to change, along with many others.

CHAPTER 17

Return from Paringa

1998

The short journey back to Cait's house and welcome company was a pleasant change from the recent turmoil of the last few days. Yes, the nurse was right he was getting a bit too old for chaotic adventures in the wilds of the west coast alpine region, yes forty or fifty years ago, but not today. Arriving at the house Cait parked round the back by the paddock, then helping Hector out of the jeep, they chatted as they walked to the back door leading into the kitchen. Both were delighted to find Rhys waiting for them with three cold beers set up on the kitchen table. While Cait took over in the kitchen and sipping her welcome cold drink, the men moved through into the living room with their beers and sat down, comfortable in each other's company chatting about nothing in particular. Hector finally put down his empty bottle, and smiled at Rhys.

'Sweet,' he said, thanking him, and was soon sound asleep.

The aroma of roast lamb from the kitchen smelt heavenly, rousing Hector from his slumbers. Delicious, after living on biscuits for the last couple of days. Soon all three were tucking in to their meal, enjoying every tasty morsel, with the mashed potatoes soaking up the delicious mint flavoured gravy. Cait then served small meringues shells with whipped cream and kiwi fruit, and for Hector it all seemed too good to be true. After all the clearing and washing up was finished, Rhys and Cait joined a drowsy Hector in the living room. Finishing off with coffee, the three started planning the trip over to Christchurch the next day, though Cait expressed that she felt another day's rest would be better for Hector.

However, he was as keen to get back home as Rhys was to collect the new, well to him, Toyota Hilux, and not lose another day's work. So, it was decided, against her better judgement, that Rhys would pick up Hector's own car first thing, then head off East straight after breakfast. Promising to contact his doctor as soon as he was home, seemed to pacify Cait.

'She'll be alright.' Rhys added smiling.

An early night followed, with all three sleeping soundly. Rising at dawn Cait made large mugs of hot tea and toast, before Rhys went to collect Hector's Honda. Helping to pack Hector's few bits and pieces into the boot and Hector into the passenger seat, Cait wished them a safe journey. A trip of one hundred and fifty two-miles, first through Arthur's Pass, then crossing the Canterbury Plain, with the Southern Alps behind them silhouetted against a clear blue sky, and on to Christchurch. Rhys hoping with normal traffic and all going to plan, he could complete the return journey as well, and be back home before bedtime. Stopping only once to stretch their legs and fill up their water flasks they made good time reaching Christchurch. Parking in Hector's driveway Rhys saw him into the house, brought his bags in too before handing over the car keys. Seeing all was fine, he put the kettle on making a cup of tea for Hector before heading out to walk to the garage which wasn't too far, to collect the Ute.

After having a good look over the vehicle, a short trial run, and then chatting with the salesman attending to the business part of the purchase, Rhys looked at his watch, time he to be heading back. However, still feeling a bit guilty dropping the older fellow off and immediately heading on his way, he decided to check up on him. He knew it is what Cate would have wanted him to do, even if it did prolong his journey. Following his better instincts, he drove back to Hector's, parking on the run-in behind the

Honda, then knocked on the door a couple of times and waited.

A bit surprised, as he wasn't expecting anyone, Hector opened the door and seeing Rys, smiled, inviting him back in, asking if everything was sweet regarding his new truck.

'Oh yeah, cheers, come and have a look. Just wondered if you needed anything and will be ok before I set off again. Cait will be asking, no doubt about that.'

'Look come in and sit-down Rhys, I'll make you a cup of tea this time, sorry I can't offer you cake or anything, a bit low on provisions.'

'Look, what if I go to the local store and pick up a few things, milk, cheese, eggs, cold meat, bread maybe? Think it would be a good idea. I'll phone Cait when I come back to keep her posted, she won't mind. Probably happy to have some time on her own for a change. Have you a spare bed, I'm sure you have?'

While Rhys was away, Hector checked the spare bed, found clean towels in the hall cupboard and laid a couple on top of the bed. No sign that his step son had slept over while he was away, so that was good. He went back into the living room starting to tidy the table, slowly, now that he only had the proper use of one arm. Never mind he was getting used to it, and would need to remember to go to the surgery tomorrow to hand in the letter and top up his prescription as well. Rhys wasn't away long and soon both men were sitting at the table enjoying cold meat and tomato sandwiches, before starting on the cream cakes, washing it all down with plenty of warm sweet tea. It had been a long day, but a successful one, for both. Cait too felt happier when Rhys phoned saying he was going to stay over, and had been out shopping for Hector too, saying she would report to the medical centre tomorrow on Hector's progress, and hoped he would remember to hand in his letter to the surgery and collect his prescription.

Both sitting contentedly, Hector on his La-Z-Boy chair and Rhys on the brown leather sofa his legs stretched out, happily sipping beers. It was then Hector decided to show Rhys the airmail letter. Reading it but saying nothing, except occasionally looking over at Hector who held his quizzical gaze, he finally folded the letter and handed it back.

'Well, well, well, that's a surprise, a bolt out of the blue, I guess. Did you know?'

'Yes, I did know.'

'You knew, but you never told anyone, did you, ever?'

'No, I didn't, though Ethel my mother knew. She had a lovely studio photograph of Lizzie holding our baby daughter, which Lizzie herself had sent over from Scotland. I think it was passed on to one of Ethel's daughters in Motueka, but heaven knows where it is now. Anyway, my daughter and I are in contact, regularly now, since that first phone call. Writing, phoning, faxing and I believe she is planning to come over to New Zealand to meet me.' Pausing, added, 'So I need to get myself sorted out.'

'Why were you down the Paringa camping and not at the bach, seems a bit strange? Did you not want anyone to know you were down?'

'Yip. Years ago, back when I was deer culling, my cobber Alan and I stumbled across a small gold seam in the rain forest just above the Paringa. We were always going to go back, but white baiting and life got in the way, then Alan was killed in a plane crash and I cleanly forgot, or really, just put it to the back of my mind. Till now.'

'Come on man, you're not forty, even sixty anymore, you're getting on, you've just lost your wife, what were you thinking about for heaven's sake?

'Yeah, I know, you're right. Cath and I had quite an argument over the letter when it arrived years ago, we never sorted it out. In fact, she took the letter and I thought she had destroyed it, but no, she had hidden it. I came across it after she died. I really felt as if I had been given a second chance.'

'Well ok, I think I see where you are coming from.' Rhys finally replied.

'I now, not only have a daughter, but a son in law, grandsons and great grandchildren, living thousands of miles away across the world. I would like to go back to the UK and meet them, before it is too late. You know Rhys, I did go back after the war in 1947. I was shore based at the Wireless Telegraph station at Waiouru, 'River of the West' you know, North Island. Originally a sheep station, and since the war an army training area in the middle of nowhere. We wrote regularly Lizzie and I. Eventually I told her I was coming back for them, even had naval accommodation organised. When I reach Gibraltar, there was a 'Dear John' letter waiting for me, she had met someone else, and had given our daughter away. Hell, was that difficult to take in. Anyway, that was the last I heard, for what, forty years, till I received the airmail letter one day from my daughter. I didn't, I couldn't reply, because the letter had disappeared. There was no reasoning with Cath, she was so, so jealous. Well, there you are Rhys, now you know.'

Hector stretched into his back pocket and brought out his wallet, handing it to Rhys saying, 'Look in there, the photo I always carry, she's lovely, isn't she? Lizzie, my daughter's mother.'

'Yes, she is Hector, I am sorry, I, we had no idea.'

'Well Rhys, turns out neither had I. She was already married, though never wore a wedding ring. Poor buggar was in the Navy too, it turned out, seldom home. Only time we nearly collided was when I had compassionate leave to visit Lizzie and our new daughter near Hexham. Seems he had returned to Rothesay looking for Lizzie, to be told by her mother that he would be far better off without her, she wasn't good enough for him. Anyway, he turned up at the nursing home, saw mother and baby and after a few choice words, left. Then I turned up, having walked miles through the snow, and my god Rhys, what did I know about babies, nothing. Boy, were we foolish, thinking about it now, and yes, you can blame the war, the lives we were living, but hell, this was a new wee life, not her fault.'

'It's not been easy for you, has it? Time for another beer?' suggested Rhys.

Both men sat back comfortably, each with their own thoughts, relishing their beer. The older man wondering if he would ever meet his new found daughter, realising that yes, he had been foolish, and yes, the injury could have been a lot worse, even fatal. The younger man struggling to make some sense of the strange accident and rescue recently down the Paringa. Hector's injury, and all he had learnt this evening, were they not all somehow connected? Finishing his beer, he stood up and took the empty bottles over to the kitchen worktop, he would tidy them away in the morning. Turning, he looked over at Hector, saying he would call it a night and thought he should do the same. It had been a long and tiring day for both of them.

CHAPTER 18

August 1945

The Long Farewell

In the summer of 1944, Hector had been transferred to the submarine base at Blyth in Northumberland on the North East Coast of England, carrying out patrols in the North Sea. The Norwegian fjords with their narrow inlets and steep mountainous backdrops offered unique protection to the German U-boats based in occupied Norway from spring 1940 to 1945. Some 240 U-boats were stationed in the Nordic country over this period. These deadliest of ships' predators lurking beneath the Atlantic and Arctic Oceans, and the North Sea, had brought Britain to within three weeks of starvation during World War 1. Soon forming the bulk of German forces engaged in the Atlantic in World War 11, U-boats were fast enough to outrun the merchant convoys. However, by June 1944 U-boats ceased using French ports, and along with the westward drive of the Soviet Red Army expelling them from the Baltic Sea, they eventually only operated out of Norway.

Learning she was pregnant, Lizzie, though not alone being pregnant at this time nor married to the baby's father, decided to move to Hexham, renting a room to be with Hector, who was based at Blyth, when he had shore leave, and planning to find a job in a local tearoom. The couple lived there throughout the autumn and winter of 1944, their daughter being born one snowy morning in January in 1945, during one of his forays in the North Sea. He received the news by telegraph and on return to base was entitled to a few days leave. Travelling by local bus to Hexham he then managed to plough his way through the snow to Dilston Hall where Lizzie and the baby were, before they moved back in to their one rented room in Hexham. Not long after this, Hector was transferred back to Scotland, this time to Dunoon. Dunoon, the main town on the Cowal peninsula in southern Argyll, situated on the eastern shore of the upper Firth of Clyde. It was here during World War11 as part of the main Clyde defences, an anti-submarine boom was anchored from the shore in Dunoon to the Cloch Point Lighthouse across the river three miles southwest of Gourock. South of Dunoon, Palmerston Fort provided one of the coastal defence gun emplacements, covering the anti-submarine boom and the open waters of the Clyde, the other gun emplacement was on top of Castle Hill above Dunoon.

Again, living in a rented room, the little family stayed out the last weeks of the war. Their landlady offering to look after the baby to allow Lizzie and Hector to take the ferry across to Gourock, then the train into Glasgow on the 8th of May, Victory in Europe day, to mark the end of nearly six years of warfare. Glaswegians could breathe easily, after knowing fearful night raids, losing loved ones at sea, *HMS Hood*, or at the front line, in combat. Even the sun shone brightly as they celebrated like thousands of others in Glasgow's George Square, in the shadow of the City Chambers, singing and jiving, before returning to Dunoon on the last ferry. The celebrations carried on for several days, as they did all over the country.

Life went on normally for Hector at the submarine base, till the morning of the 6th August 1945 when the American B-29 bomber *Enola Gay* dropped an atomic bomb on the Japanese city of Hiroshima, killing around 80,000 people, with more than tens of thousands dying later of radiation exposure. Three days later on the 9th August a second B-29 bomber dropped another atomic bomb, this time on the city of Nagasaki, killing an estimated 40,000 people. As before, in 1942, Hector was detailed to the Pacific not knowing when or if ever he would return.

Sailing out of the Clyde estuary, southwards down in the Firth this time, passing the islands of Arran and Aisla Craig, as he had in 1943 on his approach, wondering when or if he would ever see Lizzie and his baby daughter Janice again. As before, duty called, and the crew once more became family. This was indeed the long farewell.

CHAPTER 19

1950s

At Sea Again

Returning to his homeland at the end of his tour of duty in the Pacific, Hector, after leaving the base in Melbourne, Australia, was seconded to the Naval Communications Station of the Royal New Zealand Navy, just south of *Waiouru* in the middle of North Island, far from the sea. It was commissioned in 1943 during the War as the *Waiouru* Wireless Telegraph station where tens of thousands of code groups were handled each day, mostly for the British Pacific Fleet in Japanese waters. In 1951 the station was designated *HMNZS Irirangi*, Māori for 'spirit voice' and it was here that Hector completed his naval service.

While at the base he sorted out housing for himself, Lizzie and their young daughter. Continuing writing to each other, making plans, till in 1948 on his trip back to Britain, stopping at Gibraltar enroute, he received his final letter from Lizzie, this time telling him she had met someone else and had given their daughter up for adoption. Despondent, yet having to continue on to Britain with little to look forward to, he then had a long wait for a return passage to New Zealand. Greatly saddened, but realising there was nothing he could do, his life had changed once again.

Back in Motueka, Ethel, so looking forward to being united with Hector's young family, was upset when Hector contacted her to let her know what had happened. She had been so excited to welcome Hector's family to New Zealand, hoping they would eventually start a new life back on South Island not far from Motueka when Hector's service life finished. He had been a very young man when he came out of Nelson College continuing his wireless telegraphy training in Auckland on HMS Philomel. It seemed a lifetime ago, so much had happened, resulting in such turmoil across a world still recovering it seemed, from the 1914-18 war. She had been so relieved when Hector had sent a couple of messages via The Nelson Evening Mail saying he was safe and well, and now he was coming home.

Returning to Motueka, settling in took some time. Hector missed the close companionship of the last nine years. Remembering after his father had died and he and Ethel had moved to Motueka, before he went to Nelson College, he had helped unload fish from the boats at the harbour in the evenings, making pocket money to help his mother. Thinking about this he decided to go down to the harbour to see if there was any work available, even in the evenings when the fishing boats returned, helping to offload the catch. Chatting with his new 'cobbers' saying he was keen to be working again, it wasn't long before Hector set off to sea once more, joining one of Ethel's older grandsons Tommy's fishing boats, sailing off Tasman Bay, Golden Bay and Marlborough fishing grounds. They fished for a variety of fish using different fishing methods. Single trawling for snapper, gurnard, flounder, Colin dory and other bottom fish. Dredging for scallops, oysters and mussels and gillnetting for gummy sharks, like school sharks, a target species for fish and chip shops, popular because of their boneless, thick white flakes, making them ideal for the export market too.

Boxes of fish were sent to Wellington on an overnight ferry from Nelson, red snapper was exported to Japan, snapper along with other species were sent on to Australia as well as to the local markets. Fishing was seasonal, some by nature and some by regulation. Smaller boats would fish from October to January, gillnetting school shark, a target fish for fish and chip shops. Gillnetting was eventually banned, as it did unbelievable damage. It certainly captured large amounts of fish, unfortunately killing not only the targeted fish, but any sea creatures unlucky enough to swim into the nets.

From January to April, boats would head off to the west coasts of both North and South Island trolling for Albacore tuna, found in the open waters of tropical and temperate seas. The Albacore a migratory species swimming long distances throughout the oceans. By May and June, the crews were chasing Blue Fin Tuna, a dark, blue backed tuna, which meant leaving the Bays to head up and down the west coast for three months or so, heading into Greymouth and Westport if the weather was bad. The boats, only forty footers, so not best out in a storm in the sea off Greymouth, known as a 'shitty bar', and to be avoided during an outgoing, ebb tide, when the waves are most dangerous, increasing the risk of swamping. Hector said this was the most exciting fishing. Very hard work, getting tossed about in 70 knot storms, 60 miles out in the Tasman Sea, dodging Japanese and Korean trawlers in the dark, as well as the long hours trying to outsmart the fish.

One night around midnight, while the crew were resting, the fishing boat hanging on a sea anchor, a parachute deployed in the sea, allowing the forty-footer to move in a hurry, The skipper, Tommy, getting up out of his bunk for a drink of water, realised something was amiss, so started the engine, putting on all the lights which alerted the crew, just as a Japanese trawler pulled their helm hard over, their stern missing the local boat by about thirty meters. The fishermen asleep in the other trawler would have been tossed out of their bunks, as it lay a huge list to port during this manoeuvre. The thrust from its propellor lay the local boat on a 45-degree list to starboard, but not an issue fortunately, as the 40-footer could roll further with ease. Thankfully the keen-eyed seaman on the bridge of the Japanese vessel prevented what otherwise would have been a fatal disaster. Later, one evening recalling the near escape over a beer in the Returned Servicemen's club in Motueka, Hector said he got the feeling the Japanese were still after him having escaped with his life in '43 after their attack on the Achilles.

In May and June some of their other boats were engaged in dredging for Oysters and Mussels in Tasman Bay, later slipping the boats in for an annual survey and paint. By July and on into October was the scallop season, making the biggest and quickest income, helping to pay the large bills collected on survey. Many Motueka fishermen however, did own larger boats, sailing out of Nelson and Timaru, even Auckland, to fish around the world, sailing to South American ports, to Madagascar and some south to Georgia and Antarctica. It was here in the cold waters of the South Atlantic, and South Pacific oceans, Toothfish was found on the seamounts and continental shelves around the subantarctic islands. Toothfish growing to over two metres long and weighing around 100kg became rich in oil in the cold waters of the south Atlantic and Antarctic. A highly sought after, high quality white fish, again with few bones, producing a high income for the men who braved these, at times, perilous seas.

CHAPTER 20

1955

From the Depths to the Heights

Hector working several seasons on the fishing boats, was earning good money and able to help his mother Ethel. Paying rent and enjoying many a beer with local friends, fishermen like himself and returned servicemen. One of his drinking group, Alan Rodgers, spoke to him one evening when they were enjoying a couple of refreshing Steinlagers, asking if he fancied trying something different, away from a life at sea.

'Well yeah, a life at sea is all I have known Alan, war and peace. What are you suggesting, seems you've got something on your mind?'

'I am suggesting an equally rugged life, but in the Southern Alps, deer culling. The government is looking for good, keen, strong-minded men, crack shots, to keep the numbers of red deer under control. They are concerned about the increasing erosion in the high country, and rightly or wrongly the deer are blamed.'

'Yeah, ok, right, go on, sounds different, could be interesting.'

'Well, the Department of Internal Affairs, who took over the management of deer, are employing more teams of cullers. Living in small groups, in tented camps or in rough wooden huts high up in isolated parts of the Alps, killing and skinning deer. The wages are good, and there is a bonus for each skin. You'll realise of course it is hard work, but then so is fishing, so no hardship there. The days are long, and you are at the mercy of the weather as you would expect, much the same as you are at sea. What do you think?'

Alan went up to the bar to buy another couple of beers, and chat to a couple of cobbers, leaving Hector mulling over the proposition. Knowing a bit about the history, that around two hundred and fifty or so red deer, originating in Britain, were brought over from Victoria in Australia and liberated on both islands. Red deer, the most widespread breed, interbred with the Wapiti, introduced to New Zealand as a gift from American President Theodore Roosevelt in the early 1900s, and now occupying over two thousand kilometres in northern Fiordland. Then, throughout the Southern Alps, Chamois, were gifted by Emperor Franz Josef of Austria, around the same time. Soon sports shooting became a tourist attraction, greatly encouraged by the government, and by the 1920s, the golden years for deerstalking, the English gentry were targeting trophies, while the locals instead were poaching the deer for the table.

By the 1930s teams of deer cullers, employed by Internal Affairs, signalled the era of the professional hunter. To begin with, there was no shortage of potential cullers keen to give this life a try, though it wasn't long before many were quitting, realising quite soon, they were not tough enough or strong enough for the rough life. Especially when winter loomed high in the Alps, and soon warm log fires and tasty home cooking seemed by far the better choice.

Hector however, was convinced he was strong enough to endure this way of life. Having faced Japanese bombers on the Pacific, German U-boats in the North Sea and Arctic Ocean, depth charges from German battleships, surely, he would be able to cope with New Zealand winters high in the Alps. So, by the end of his third beer or maybe even his fourth, he was ready to sign on the dotted line. A few days later all was signed and sealed in Nelson. Letting his nephew know he was moving on and his mother Ethel too, that he was off again on another adventure, explaining that this time he would manage home on a more regular basis, so she wasn't to worry, and yes, he would take care of himself.

Setting off, Alan and Hector filled the truck with a couple of sleeping bags, warm clothes, cooking pots, tins of canned food, and anything else they thought they would need for the next couple of months. Keen to start now that everything was organised, they made their way from Motueka to join the main road at Matupika and on to Murchison, stopping off for a bite to eat at a friend's house, bringing him up to date with his latest plan. They drove on via Irangahua to Reefton, before heading to the coast at Greymouth. From there following on down the coastal route to Hokitika, they overnighted at a navy pal's house, enjoying a few beers, his wife making them a warm dinner, their last taste of home cooking for a while. Next morning after a hearty breakfast their friend drove them over to the airbase, dropping them off along with their equipment, before driving Alan's truck back to park in his yard, ready for their return. Flying south from Hokitika to their base in the Westland area above Fox Glacier, on the western approaches of the Southern Alps between Mount Cook and Mount Huxley, which would be their hunting ground. Again, here he was, as far as probable from civilization. He did wonder how Lizzie and his now ten-year-old daughter Janice were, and how they would have fitted into the life he was now leading. Here, in this Alpine wilderness, as out on the ocean fishing, you had to keep your wits about you constantly, no time to think about what might have been, it was the moment that counted.

CHAPTER 21

On his own again

Christchurch late 1990s

Rhys was up bright and early having slept reasonably well, considering all the beer and heartfelt conversation of the previous evening. He switched the kettle on, toasted two slices of the bread he had bought the previous evening and boiled a couple of eggs. Setting the table, remembering to put out butter and marmalade too, he was presently aware he had company.

'Morning old boy, how are you? Sleep well?'

'Yip, sure did, but less of the 'old boy'. How about you?' Pausing before adding, 'Sorry about me rambling on and on last night, not like me. Hope you didn't mind?'

'No, of course I didn't mind, more surprised, I guess. Quite a lot to take in, but no I didn't mind. How about you? Guess it was good to explain everything and get it off your chest. Any time.'

The buzzer went for the eggs. Rhys, put them in the egg cups and placed them on the table. Hector lifted the toast from the toaster and Rhys brought the tea over, then finally they sat down. Again in companionable silence they ate their breakfast.

After clearing and tidying up, Rhys said he would have to be on his way. However, there were a few things he needed to get straight, like Hector assuring him he would call in at the surgery with his letter from the medical centre, and promising he would phone in the evening to let Caitlin know how he had got on. Filling a bottle of water, and wrapping up a hastily made cheese sandwich, Rhys said his goodbyes. Heading out of the city this time in his new Toyota, and for once actually looking forward to his trip across the plain to Arthur's Pass. He had a lot to think about, a lot to tell Caitlin too, wondering if she would believe him.

'Were you two drinking a few beers, maybe more than a few by the sounds of it? Not so good if Hector was remembering taking his medication. No wonder he had tales to tell.' He could hear Caitlin say.

Closing the door, the house quiet again, Hector remembered there was still some tea in the pot, so refilling his cup he sat down. No sooner had he finished the tea, and put his cup down, than he fell asleep. He woke with a start, remembering he had his tablets to take and the surgery to go to. Shaving and tidying himself as best he could with his one good arm, though he was becoming more adept now, he checked his pockets for his wallet. Picking up the Doctor's letter he put it in his jacket pocket, then struggled a bit to put the jacket on. Lifting up the house keys, closing and locking the door behind him, he made his way to the surgery. It wasn't far and he took his time. The main thing on his mind was how to explain his accident to the Doctor.

'Play it by ear.' he said to himself, not knowing of course what had been written in the letter by the staff in Hokitika.

'Good morning, Hector,' the receptionist said with a bright smile, 'come away in and sit down, Doctor will be with you shortly. Nice to see you again. Been in the wars I see.'

Hector handed over the letter, and went and sat down. Shortly the Doctor came through, the receptionist handing him Hector's letter. Glancing quickly at the letter, he then looked up and seeing Hector, smiled, asking him to come through to the consulting room.

'So, a bit of an accident, well let me have a look. You were certainly lucky, could have been a lot worse.'

Changing the dressing and helping him on with the sling, he said to Hector to make another appointment but for the nurse next time to check and change his dressing.

'However, if you have any bother with your arm or shoulder before, just phone. How are you managing on your own Hector since your wife died, a few months now is it?'

'Yes, I was getting along fine, even decided to take a trip down the West coast for a few days, till this happened. Real careless. Maybe not just as over things as I thought, or had hoped.'

Thanking the Doctor, Hector went back through to the receptionist to make the next appointment then headed home. The first thing he did when he went into the house was put the kettle on. He felt he should make himself a sandwich, breakfast seemed a while ago, and it was nearly lunch time, where had the morning gone?

He was just about to sit down with his mug of tea and ham sandwich when there was a sharp knock at the front door. Putting his mug down on the coffee table, he went over to the door, but before he had opened it there was another even sharper, louder knock. Opening the door, Hector found a man and a woman standing, and presumed it was their vehicle parked behind his on the driveway. Introducing themselves as Detective Senior Sergeant McIntyre and Detective Constable Sands of Canterbury CIB, Christchurch, he asked if they could come in. Stepping back to allow the two officers in, he closed the door and invited them into the living room offering them a seat. Hector sat down too.

'I am more than surprised to see you, how can I help you?' Hector started.

'We have been recently contacted by the CIB in Greymouth regarding a recent accident on the banks of the Paringa river.' Pausing before adding, 'I believe you have recently been down the west coast Mr Crichton, and that you have a bach or holiday home by the river? You also fish for whitebait there in season, but not this visit?' enquired the DSS as he took notes.

'Quite right, it is not in season. Yes, I was down the coast but not at the bach. I haven't been down since my wife died in mid-summer. Saying that, I will need to go down and tidy up a few things soon, before winter sets in. Seems to come round quicker each year.' His mind racing.

Writing it down the officer continued, 'I notice you appear to have injured your arm, can you tell me how that happened?'

'Oh, shooting possum, tripped and fell and the gun went off, lucky really.' The lie tripping off his tongue so easily, he amazed himself. Both officers watched him closely.

'Tricky I would have thought, out in the wilds of the rain forest with a rifle, hunting at your age, is it not, especially on your own?'

'I know the area well, I used to be a deer culler in the Southern Alps years ago, long before I was married, or had the bach. I felt like a few days away, camping in a secluded area I knew well, and maybe a bit of prospecting too. There's the odd small gold seam around there if you know where to look.' Best being a bit truthful, Hector thought.

'Prospecting? Any luck?' The DSS kept his eyes fixed on Hector.

'No, no luck, as you can see, pointing at his arm.' Hector held the officer's gaze.

'Who knew you were away prospecting? Or did you not tell anyone, perhaps keeping it a secret?'

'No, not a secret, but yes, you are right, I didn't tell anyone. As I said, I just wanted some time away on my own.'

Looking round the living room and adjoining kitchen, the Senior Detective then asked, 'Do you live alone Mr Crichton? I am asking because I see two sets of dishes on the draining board.'

'Yes, I do live alone since my wife died. But yes, the friend who drove me over from the coast yesterday stayed last night, we got talking and enjoyed a few beers. He also did a bit of food shopping for me, and made sure I was ok this morning before he left. He drove back over in my car yesterday as I can't drive.' He touched his arm.

'Worked out well really, as he was collecting his new Ute this morning in town before heading back west. So, suited us both. His name is Rhys Hughes, he lives in Hokitika, his wife Caitlin is a distant relative of my late wife.'

DSS McIntyre wrote quickly, taking down every word. Det Sands watched and listened; not wanting to miss anything. Although her boss was leading the enquiry and taking down the notes, she knew he would ask later if she had noticed anything in particular, that she might want to add. She was still in training; keen to learn, and wanting to keep in her senior officer's good books.

Looking up DSS McIntyre continued, 'Did you and your wife have any family Mr Crichton?'

Hector paused before replying, wondering where the questioning was going. 'Yes and no. We did and we didn't so to speak.'

'I don't understand, please explain, Mr Crichton.'

'Well, my late wife was a widow when we met, and had an only son. He is married now and lives with his wife a few miles south of here.'

'And you, do you have any family of your own?'

'Officer, why are you asking me all these questions, why are you here? What have I done? I told you where I have been, and how I injured myself. Now if there is nothing else, I would like you to leave now as I have had a difficult couple of days and the painkillers prescribed by the doctor are making me feel quite bushed.'

DSS McIntyre stood and put his notebook and pencil in his pocket, then nodding to the young Detective said, 'OK I understand, that will be all for today, I do realise you have had a difficult time Mr Crichton.'

The CIB officer turned as he reached the door, thanking Hector for his time, adding he would be back in touch again, as the Greymouth CIB would have other relevant questions they would want answered. Hector paused by the door, repeating to himself, 'relevant questions', wonder what he means by that? He watched, as they reversed their vehicle out of the driveway, wondering what that was all about. Closing and locking the door, Hector suddenly felt very tired. Without even bothering with the sandwich still on the worktop making himself a fresh cup of tea, he went off to bed and slept soundly.

It was nearly dark when he came to, and the phone was ringing. By the time he reached the phone whoever it was had hung up. He checked the time, it was eight in the evening, what had happened to the day? Slowly things began to fall in to place; Rhys, the visit to the surgery, then the police. He put a light on and made his way to the kitchen, boy was he hungry. Hell, breakfast was the last time he had eaten, and his arm was aching, time for some painkillers, but better eat first, but what? The phone rang again, he picked it up, it was Rhys to let him know he had got home safely, and checking to see how he was.

'All fine this end,' Hector said, 'and glad to hear you are home. Pleased with your purchase? Behaved well I take it? That's good. Thanks again for your help Rhys, it was much appreciated, and I will be in touch soon. All the best to Caitlin, thank her again for her help, especially the great dinner.' The mention of it was too much. 'Rhys, thanks again, but I need to go.' And hardly taking a breath added, 'Yes, I'll let you know how things are, bye for now.'

Realising he had been a bit offhand, he felt bad, especially after all they had done for him. He knew he should be eating more than a sandwich, taking note to take some meat out the freezer tomorrow, but a sandwich would have to do tonight along with a mug of tea, hot this time. After finishing his meagre supper, he did feel a bit better. He took another painkiller, then after tidying round and a quick wash headed back to bed. Tomorrow was another day. Lying in bed his mind wandering, going over everything and thinking again it was strange he hadn't heard from his step son for a few weeks, not that he was too bothered really. Putting the light out, and mentally adding 'phone call to Neil' to the list in his head. He was not looking forward to it; along with everything else he had to do.

CHAPTER 22

Westlands - South Island

late 1959-1960s

The deer culling life suited Hector. The winters on the snow-covered peaks were no great hardship. A Christmas dinner of porridge boiled in a tin can over an open wood fire suited him fine. Alan and he kept their strength up by butchering and cooking the odd deer. They met their targets, and by strange coincidence met Sir Edmund Hillary. Mountaineering in their block one day, having not long returned home from his conquest of Everest. Later that evening by their camp fire Hector and Alan talked over their extraordinary meeting, wondering if anyone would believe them next time they were back in civilization enjoying a pint in their local Both returned home for visits, but were always keen to return to the wilds. It was during one midwinter that Hector received a message from one of the other deer cullers who had just returned from leave, saying he had heard that Hector's mother Ethel was not keeping well and would like to see her son soon again.

A chopper flight and land rover were arranged and Hector made his way back to Motueka to spend time with Ethel, realising very quickly she was nearing her end, she was ninety years old. Living with her granddaughter and family during her final days, the local nurse attending her, Hector who had a bed at a friend's house came in early in the morning to sat with his mother, holding her hand and quietly reminiscing over their life together with his father Robert, back on the farm in Dovedale. Recalling going off to Nelson College, his training on the Philomel, his father's old ship, and meeting Dolly for the first time in Christchurch. Ethel eventually drifting in and out of consciousness, managing only to sip a little water, struggled to say that he should try to find his daughter. She had kept the photo she had safely, and wanted him to have it. Smiling he told Ethel he loved her and thanked her for all she had done for him, for their life together. Sadly, realising she could no longer hear him, he kissed her hand and held it close to his heart.

Her funeral was a simple family gathering in the local cemetery. Huddled together to keep warm against flurries of snow and the chill wind coming off snow-covered Mount Arthur. The family listened to the minister's words of comfort as they laid their mother, grandmother, great grandmother and friend to rest. Each with their own thoughts of Ethel, whose own father had arrived in New Zealand back in 1842 sailing from Portsmouth, England; Portsmouth where one hundred years later Hector's own life had changed so dramatically. As each member of the family threw a flower onto Ethel's coffin, saying their last goodbye, Hector silently promised his mother he would try and find his daughter, though when, where and how, he did not know.

In a few days Hector headed back down the coast. Feeling quite alone for the first time since his father died back in 1930, he wondered where life would now lead him. He would miss Ethel. However, meeting up with Alan and appreciating the few bottles of Speight's and Lion Red he had brought back with him, he realised life does indeed go on, but at least you have your memories

July passed, as did August, and in September on the west coast, many kiwis made their way down the Paringa to make extra money fishing for whitebait. It was during one season while he and Alan headed down the coast to do some fishing, he met Cath, a widow with a young son. They came down every year from Hokitika for the fishing, staying in her bach which was simple. Alan and Hector agreeing to give her a hand to improve and extend the property in exchange for a bed each and shelter during their visits to the coast. They added a simple shower, an outside covered storage area for the two canoes and the fine net covered bulky box like whitebait fishing gear, and a shed for the quadbike. It was a good life and good money, along with the deer culling. Sadly, it was during one of the white baiting seasons that tragedy struck. Alan was killed in a helicopter crash returning with boxes of fish to Hokitika.

Hector decided then to give up the deer culling and head back to Motueka when the season was over in November. Till then he continued to help Cath with the fishing and the bach. He started planting a small garden to grow some vegetables around the side and front of the property, putting up a wooden fence to keep out the few wandering cows. He mended nets, and every evening took boxes of fresh fish up to the bridge for collection in the horse and cart. Their working partnership grew into friendship, both later deciding perhaps they should get married. Cath's reason being it would be good for her young son to have a proper father figure about the place again. So, all thoughts of his promise of finding his daughter slipped from his mind and he started a new life, with a wife and step son.

First, they decided to stay over on the west coast permanently at Fox, building a general store and tearoom with living accommodation, the store becoming the hub of local life. This became their life and they thrived on the West coast. Renting out the bach during part of the whitebait season to family and friends, and during summer holidays to tourists to add to their income. Hector also kept busy keeping not only the shop and tearoom in good order but the bach too, along with all the fishing equipment and the little garden. During the school holidays Neil helped his step father, who took him fishing and possum hunting. Hector had made a secure gun cabinet for the two rifles he owned and Neil enjoyed hunting in the rain forest with Hector, which he much preferred to fishing. Learning to ride the quad bike along the beach was also exciting, though

Cath was always concerned, accidents happened so easily. However, she knew Hector would keep Neil right and was happy that they seemed to get along together. Visits to Motueka in the north of South Island became few and far between. Then after several years of living and working down the coast, after much discussion, the decision was made to move back east to Christchurch. Cath's son was growing up, schooling was better in the city and there were more opportunities as the fishing life it seemed did not appeal to him.

Moving east they bought a small holding north of Christchurch around Kaipoi, growing soft fruits for the market, mainly strawberries. Hector bought a larger truck and extended the store at the side of their property to house his new truck and the packing boxes. Still, every September till November they carried on the tradition of white baiting, meeting up with old friends and family on the west coast and managed to keep the bach and grounds in good order.

Realising that the seasonal fruit picking was leaving time on his hands, Hector took a job at the freezer works, having gained his experience for this type of work during his years culling in the Southern Alps.

And so, the seasons moved on and the years passed.

CHAPTER 23

Christchurch late 1990s

Hanging up the phone having tried unsuccessfully to call his stepson; Hector was relieved in a way there was no reply. Yet was beginning to wonder why there was no answer, having tried phoning at different times over the last week. Beginning to feeling better in himself, his arm virtually back to normal, he decided instead to catch up with some gardening which had been neglected since his accident. Able to go into town in the car again, and do some food shopping, he felt he was getting back to some sort of normality. Of course, he realised things would be different now that Cath died, knew he would manage, he always did.

The phone rang at the same moment a car turned into the driveway. Looking up from deadheading the roses which filled the border at the side of the drive, he immediately recognised the driver and his young female companion. The phone continued ringing, but instead of going to answer, he stood waiting on his visitors. The phone stopped ringing. Hector felt he had no option but to invite the two officers in, rather than leave them standing out in the front garden, knowing it would encourage the neighbours to indulge in a bit of speculation. Once in the living room all three sat down, the sense of deja vu apparent.

'Pleased to see you seem to be keeping better, busy too Mr Crichton. Have you given some thought to our previous visit?' DSS McIntyre enquired, pausing, then adding, 'I am afraid I have some bad news for you. I am now at liberty to tell you it seems a younger man has been badly injured down the Paringa, at, or about the same time you were in the area prospecting. The accident happened close to your property; on the same day you were injured. A bit of a coincidence, don't you think?'

'Not really, why do you think that?' Hector responded. 'I knew nothing of an accident, though I vaguely remember hearing a helicopter flying over when I was lying on the ground, after tripping over when the gun went off. It puzzled me because I didn't know anyone knew about my accident, far less that I was in the vicinity, and my flight out I knew had been arranged for the following day. I blacked out several times if I remember, so never heard the helicopter again. Actually, I forgot about it. Sorry I can't be of more help.'

'I take it you haven't been back down the coast to your property since you returned home?' the officer said, continuing to take notes.

'No, that's right, I haven't. I have only recently started driving again and it's a bit of a hike for me to drive over to the coast. Tom Connal, the water bailiff, however keeps an eye on things for me and I am sure he would have been in touch he had noticed anything out of the ordinary.'

At that moment the phone rang, penetrating the now daunting atmosphere in the room. No one moved. McIntyre, realising that Hector was not making an attempt to answer it, stood up saying,

'Are you going to get the phone, Mr Crichton, or will I?

'Oh sorry, I didn't think you would want to be disturbed, I am sure it is nothing.'

Two strides and the DSS lifted the receiver, listened, then handed it over, 'It's for you.

'Yeah, Hector here.'

The one-sided conversation taking less than a minute, paled Hector's face. He was clearly shocked.

Yeah, nah, let me phone you back, I have company at the moment. But look, why am I only hearing about this now?'

Not waiting for an answer he pushed himself up out of the chair, and walking over put the phone back on its cradle Tottering back to his seat, he kept his eyes lowered.

'Make Mr Crichton a cup of tea Detective Sands, please, in fact make one for each of us.'

The young Det busied herself in the kitchen, boiling water, looking for clean mugs, spoons, milk, not forgetting plenty of sugar. Placing the tray on the coffee table between them, the three unlikely associates were soon sipping hot sweet tea, each with their own thoughts. Hector stirred repeatedly, wondering what else could happen, what other questions he was going to be asked. His mind actively anticipating what his answers might be.

The two men's eyes locked. 'You seem troubled, disturbed, Mr Crichton, was it bad news?'

'Yeah, it was.' Hector replied. 'Very bad news'.

'Care to enlighten us?'

Young Det Sands put her cup down, topping up Hector's tea, and adding just a drop of milk but two more sugars, stirring it for him this time, as the senior officer picked up his pencil and notebook once again, waiting on the older man's reply.

'Well, it seems my late wife's son has been badly injured in a quad bike accident, so badly so, he is paralysed. He is in Christchurch Hospital. That was his wife, Lynn, who phoned just now.

'Have you seen or been in touch with him recently?' inquired DSS McIntyre

'No, as I said not recently, a few weeks anyway, when he came round to collect some things belonging to his mother which he said he wanted, or perhaps his wife wanted, I didn't ask. Ornaments, vases, tea sets, and family photographs.

Glancing round, Det Sands saw there were still quite a few ornaments, a crystal vase or two, and several silver trophies in the large display cabinet, perhaps he had been planning a return visit, if and when the house was empty.

Continuing, Hector then remembered, 'I also noticed quite a few bits and pieces missing out of the garage which he has always had his eye on, and are no longer there. But I hadn't realised they had been taken till yesterday. My neighbour Jim often borrows bit and bobs, but always asks, he has no access to my garage anyway, so I just supposed my stepson had taken them.'

'Sorry to hear this Mr Crichton, must have been a shock for you. A bit strange you are only hearing now. Am I right in thinking you might not have seen eye to eye with your stepson, especially now that his mother has died?'

'Oh, the usual, I guess. Only son, maybe resented me over the years, though he was fairly young when his father died, so guess I was the only father he really had. We had some good times down the river though, with his young cousins as well, canoeing, fishing, possum hunting, quad biking and panning for gold along the Tasman shore line.'

'So, he could handle himself pretty well, quad biking, firing a rifle?

'Yip, pretty well. He came with me into the bush when I went hunting possum, the odd deer, yeah learning to stock prey and handle a rifle. Became pretty sharp. However, you know what boys and young men are like, need to be watched.'

'Not a boy or a young man now, Mr Crichton, a grown man with a mind of his own, a bit of a temper even.'

'Yeah, you are right there.'

Both officers studied Hector, not really surprised at his reply.

The Detective Senior Sergeant stood up, thanking Hector before making his way to the door, Det Sands following.

At the door McIntyre turned saying, 'You have had a bit of a shock Mr Crichton, take care, take time to let it all sink in. Here's my card, if there is anything you remember or feel you need to discuss, call this number, anytime. Saying that however, we will be back in touch.'

Why? Hector said to himself as he closed the door. Picking up the tray of empty cups, he carried them over to the kitchen sink planning to wash and tidy up later. He couldn't be bothered either going back out into the front garden to finish pruning, though realised he might have felt better being out in the fresh air. It was a lot to take in. Neil's accident, sounded pretty horrific. He felt relieved in a way that Cath was no longer here to know what had happened to her son.

His ponderings were interrupted by a knock at the door. Pete Ross and Jim Watson, his next-door neighbours had come round to enquire if everything was alright. Both having spotted the car, the same car as before they thought, the police perhaps, and were just concerned. Hector said he was fine, and yes it had been the police, but he knew about as much as Pete and Jim did, so not to worry. He thanked them for coming round, but as he was about to make himself a fresh tea, sit down and watch some television, as he seemed to have been on the go all day, he would catch up with them later.

Closing the door, he had a passing thought, perhaps Jim or Pete might have noticed Neil round the house recently, yet there again maybe not if he was in Christchurch hospital. It was becoming more baffling by the minute, a lot to puzzle out. Switching on the television he decided to pour himself a beer instead of making tea, settle down and watch some cricket.

CHAPTER 24

Scotland 1945

Post War

Lizzie was struggling on her own with the baby, and her mother Annie, was keen for her to start back working in the restaurant, so Lizzie realised she would need to make a decision soon. Three of her sisters had had babies during the war and Annie said there was no room for another one, especially as Lizzie was on her own with the baby. Living in the one roomed flat up from the pier in Rothesay where she and Hector had stayed, she knew she needed to get back to work to be able to pay the rent and support herself and the baby. Realising the best thing she could do was ask her mother for help. After talking it over Annie decided the answer would be to get in touch the National Vigilance Association in Glasgow who would find a suitable home for baby Janice.

After several weeks Annie had a reply from the Superintendent at the Association that an older couple had been found, and soon the arrangement would be finalised. Lizzie, the baby, along with one of her sisters, Jean, with whom she had been staying in Cardonald, in Glasgow, over the last few weeks, took a bus into the city centre, then another bus to Garnet Hill, an area which grew up as a suburb of Glasgow in the early 19th century. The little group arrived as planned at the NVA home around lunch time, rang the bell, and were invited in by Miss McMillan, a social worker and retired nurse. After showing the trio into the waiting room, previously a large lounge of the mansion house, Miss McMillan said to Lizzie she would need to examine baby Janice. Lizzie took off the baby's clothes and handed the now whimpering Janice to Miss McMillan who after a quick examination pronounced her healthy and strong, if a bit hungry, which seemed to have gone unnoticed, especially by the anxious young mother.

Shortly afterwards the new mother arrived. Having taken the subway from St Enoch's Square, to Cowcaddens, then walking the long road up to the Home in Hill Street, on the north western edge of the city centre. Many of the villas and tenements built on the steep slopes and hills of the city, survived, however the Glasgow Observatory located nearby the Home had long been demolished.

The waiting was not easy, and by the time a rather tired but excited Margaret arrived, the young mother was crying as well as baby Janice. Miss McMillan, remembering Margaret from their nursing days in Glasgow, well over a decade and more ago, welcomed her warmly, showing her through to the main office.

There were a couple of final forms to read and sign, which didn't take long. Miss McMillan excused herself, walking back through to the large lounge, where Lizzie was sitting in the corner of the settee, nursing her now sleeping baby daughter. Jean was standing beside them, protectively resting her hand Lizzie's shoulder, comforting her. Lizzie looked up as Miss McMillan came in, who asked her to follow her through to the main office with the baby. The hardest part of all, for all, was taking the baby from Lizzie, and handing her over to her new mother. By this time Lizzie was sobbing hysterically, and baby Janice, wide awake with the disturbance and sobbing, also started howling.

As pre-arranged, a taxi was waiting outside for the new mother and baby. Miss McMillan, carrying and trying to console the sobbing baby, followed Margaret down the steps to the pavement. Seeing them, the driver came round and opened the taxi door, then waiting till Margaret was seated, she handed over baby Janice saying,

'You know my phone number Margaret, you have my card, any problems give me a call, but I am sure you will be perfectly capable, as I well remember from our Victoria Infirmary days, though that is a while ago now, what fifteen years maybe?' Both women nodded, and sharing a knowing smile, before saying goodbye.

The taxi carrying mother and baby headed down on to Sauchiehall Street, before turning right into Renfield Street, and on down to St Enoch's Square, off Argyll Street before turning left up the cobbled slope to the station entrance. Fortunately arriving in time to catch the next steam train at platform 13 to Ayr, Margaret walked as smartly as she could along the concourse, carrying the whimpering baby and handbag on one arm and ticket in her other hand which she showed to the ticket collector at the barrier. Mother and baby were just in time as the train was about to leave. Seeing her struggle the guard held the wooden door open for Margaret, and helped her up into the carriage, waiting till she sat down, before closing the door. Looking along the platform and satisfied all was well, he raised the green flag and blew the whistle. The rhythmic chugging, hissing and whistle blowing of the steam engine as it made its way out of St Enoch station to power its way down the tracks heading for the Ayrshire coast, did little to pacify baby Janice now at the start of her new life.

On the other side of the world her father was asleep in his hammock, aboard his ship on the Pacific Ocean, heading for Melbourne, Australia, unaware of what was happening to his daughter, of where she was going, and what her future held. Janice on the other hand was sucking furiously on her mother's little finger, no longer crying. Their travelling companions in the carriage looking on, undoubtedly wondering by their puzzled expressions, why the mother didn't have a bottle with her to feed the baby, who was decidedly grizzly.

Eventually and after a couple of unexpected stops along the way, between Paisley and Kilwinning, the train then stopped to drop off passengers at Irvine, Troon and Prestwick before it rumbled noisily across the railway bridge over the river Ayr, grinding slowly and deafeningly to a halt at the platform nearest the back entrance onto Station Road. By this time both exhausted, and in spite of the noise, and movement of the other passengers as they struggled passed, mother and baby were sound asleep. Margaret suddenly awoke with a start, and laid the sleeping baby on the now empty seat beside her. Standing and fastening her coat just as the guard was about to close the heavy wooden carriage door, but noticing mother and baby, he stopped and gave her a hand, helping both down on to the platform. Thanking him she walked towards the barrier where her sister-in-law Mary, was waiting. Seeing Margaret and the baby she excitedly asked the ticket collector if she could go through to help the lady with the baby.

'Oh, on you go.' he muttered, as if to add don't make a habit of it.

Thanking him, she ran through the gate on to the platform, passing the other passengers now heading home, her heels click clicking on the hard surface. Such joy on the faces of the two women as they met.

'Oh, isn't she lovely, but she must be so hungry, let's get you both home.'

Margaret handed the baby over to Mary and the two women excitedly walked home, chatting enthusiastically the whole way. It wasn't far, but over the years both recalled and wondered why they had never thought to take a taxi on such a special occasion.

Through the close, and on up the outside stair they went in the gathering dusk with their precious bundle. Margaret's hands, all fingers and thumbs, struggled to find the door key in her bag. At last managing to open the door, they went in and switched on the light in the narrow hall. Mary laid the baby in the new navy pram, all ready and waiting by the bed recess in the kitchen-living room. After taking their coats off, Mary brought the coal pail in from the large press in the hall and built up the fire, while

Margaret filled the kettle to put on the range to boil. Janice's bottle was the first priority, followed by a fresh towelling nappy, after enjoying her long awaited bottle. Settling and tucking her in her pram for a well-earned sleep, the two sisters in law at last enjoyed a very welcome cup of tea, with a homemade pancakes and jam, followed by a piece of sultana cake. It had been a long but exciting day, never to be forgotten.

Across the Firth of Clyde on Bute, Lizzie, having said a tearful goodbye to Jean also at St Enoch's station, caught the train to Wemyss Bay in time to catch the tea time ferry to Rothesay. Returning home, but to an empty flat, was less excited. Instead, she was sad, very sad, wondering if she had done the right thing.

By now Hector's watch was well under way in the South Pacific as the exceptionally traumatic day, both sad and joyous, for different reasons half a world away, was coming to a close. Hector's mother had given him away as a baby for adoption twenty-one years before, in Nelson, New Zealand.

It would be fifty-three years before he and his daughter would be reunited.

CHAPTER 25

Gourock - Scotland

1947 - 1948

One cold evening in the spring of 1947, the Royal Naval Review sailed into the Firth of Clyde, with over a hundred ships assembling at the Tail o' the Bank to anchor near Gourock. Warships, cruisers, aircraft carriers and submarines sailed through the deep waters between the Ayrshire Coast and the Island of Arran. Where Hector had sailed four years previously on his way to Rothesay Bay, across the Firth from Gourock. Two-year-old Janice carried on her father's shoulders, watched this never to be seen again, momentous, and historic sight. Her father Jim, like Hector, had been in the Royal Navy, serving in World War1 on the Atlantic Convoys, sailing out of Liverpool. At that time the Royal Navy was the world's largest and most powerful navy, and had been since Nelson's victory at Trafalgar. So yes, this was a historic moment, certainly not understood by young Janice, but recalled over the years, so stored at the back of her mind all her life. More recently her new father had been a Captain in the Home Guard in World War11, but memories of the seventeen-year-old boy high in the crow's nest signalling in the dark, out in the middle of the wild and dangerous Atlantic Ocean never left him. He wanted to share these moments with his new daughter. The Naval Review was later inspected by King George V1 and Queen Elizabeth, aboard HMS Vengeance.

The following summer of 1948 Janice and her mother Margaret set off on holiday from Renfrew Airport in a BEA De Haviland

DH89 twin winged *Dragon Rapide* flying to Kirkwall in Orkney, to join her father who was there on business, managing to fit in some trout fishing as well. So, four years after Hector was on submarine duty in Scapa Flow, his young daughter was there, in peace time. A week or so later at the end of their holiday, on their late evening return flight in a summer storm, which tested the pilot's and radio operator's skills, the *Rapide* skirted the Renfrew Heights, so close Margaret felt she could have touched the hillside from the window as the radio operator dragged in the aerial. She was ever so glad to eventually land safely back at Renfrew Airport, where a taxi was waiting to drive them back home to Ayr.

The *Rapide's* post war career to the Orkneys was short lived, as a few months later in January 1949, the DH89 flight tipped over on landing on water-logged grass on North Ronaldsay and severely damaged. Any chance of reviving air services to the Northern Isles ended, despite petitions from the islanders. However, in February 1950, at a cost of £50, and for the first time in British election history, a chartered BEA *Rapide* flew ballot boxes from Shetland to Kirkwall in Orkney, for the count. Jo Grimond was the newly elected MP, who six years later became leader of the Liberal Party in Westminster.

In 1948 Margaret decided to tell her now three-year-old daughter, before anyone else told her, that she had had another mummy who wasn't able to keep her, and so she had been adopted. Realising that Janice was having difficulty understanding the full meaning of this at such an early age, Margaret told her that she was special and had been chosen by her to be her little girl, her daughter. The idea that her first mummy had given her away, made a lasting, deep impression on her. Of being left without a mummy again led to many nights of Margaret sitting by Janice's bed, till she eventually stopped crying and fell asleep.

Growing up by the sea, the Firth of Clyde on the West coast and holidaying every year by the sea on the East coast, Janice developed a love of, not only the sea, but of small boats. Learning to row, while fishing with her father for brown trout in a reservoir in south Ayrshire, Penwhapple; Loch Ericht and Loch Garry by Dalwhinnie, again for brown trout, and when she was a bit older lobster potting, after the 'soak time' off Islay while staying in Port Askaig. Port Askaig is where the ferry from the mainland comes in from West Loch Tarbet, weather permitting. A treacherous stretch of water where ten currents meet, temperatures varying by only one degree from summer to winter, 51F/50F. Janice befriended old Archie the local ferryman, who ran the small wooden ferry trawling back and forth between Port Askaig and Feolin on Jura, a journey of ten minutes on a good day. Usually a choppy, sea-sprayed trip, but one which Janice loved, and always exciting. Part of most summers were also spent in a rented house in North Berwick on the east coast of Scotland, equally bracing. Learning to swim rain or shine in the local swimming pool by the harbour, filled with cold North Sea water, and encouraged by the New Zealand swimming instructor, a Mr Woodhead. The 'chittery' bite of a digestive biscuit at the end of the lesson always being the best bit, and no matter how much Janice chittered and complained about the cold, every morning during the holiday, into the cold water she had to jump.

Afternoons were much more to her liking, often hunting crabs among the rockpools of the east bay when the tide was out, carrying them back to the house in a bucket to be shared among the neighbours. Janice also made friends with the east coast ferryman Colin Anderson, whose little ferry boat she had noticed in the harbour beside the swimming pool. Many afternoons were spent in his wooden boat taking 'well wrapped up' holiday makers out to, and around the Bass Rock, weather permitting. The Bass, the Ailsa Craig of the East, an island, about 340 million years old, standing more than three hundred and thirty feet high in the cold waters of the outer part of the Firth of Forth, as it flows into the North Sea. A lighthouse had been constructed on the rock in 1902, which Janice could see flashing from her bedroom window. There were also the remains of an ancient chapel, but most famous is the world's largest colony of gannets, one of the largest seabirds in the Northern climes. Seals too can be spotted, along with dolphins, often racing along beside the little boat. Colin, deftly manoeuvred his craft in the usually choppy seas close to the Rock, the cold salt spray stinging everyone's faces, but hopefully avoiding the guano which covers the Bass. The close proximity allowed for amazing views of the thousands of seabirds whose constant raucous, throaty, metallic clangour was ear-splitting. A never to be forgotten experience, and for Janice, another thrilling adventure.

Back home, like Hector as a wee boy, Janice gave her mother a hand with the hens. The first two were called Bessie and Berty, after the King and Queen. They lived in a homemade wooden henhouse with tarpaulin roof at the far end of the long garden beside the Victoria plum tree. The top part of the garden was divided and fenced off and where the bantams scraped about, clucking away contentedly all day long. Janice had a little wicker basket and it was her task to gather the eggs, smaller than hens' eggs, but with lovely golden yolks. Helping too, to make and carry the hot mash for the hens at tea time, summer, winter, rain, hail or shine. When one of the bantams started to sit on eggs in the henhouse, Janice had little white china eggs to encouraged the 'cloakin' hen' to sit on, till they were exchanged for real fertilised eggs.

It was then time for Janice and her dad on a Saturday afternoon to take the red double decker bus to the terminus at Burns Monument, walk a mile or so up the road to a small holding on Carrick Hill to collect a clutch of six fertilized eggs, for the bantam to sit on and hatch. Such great excitement waiting for the first baby chick to start tapping and crack open its shell. Each tiny black and yellow chick in turn was carefully brought in to the house, put in a cosy lined and covered wicker basket by the fire to keep warm, till all the chicks were hatched. The little bundles of black and yellow fluff were then safely returned to the mother hen in her specially heated pen, till the fast-growing chicks were able to be moved outside on to the grass in their own little run with their mother. Eventually when big enough they joined the other bantams in the main run at the top of the garden

Picking plums, damsons, pears and apples too in season echoed Hector's childhood, though in a much smaller scale. After the late, very heavy snow of March 1947 with Janice building her first snowman, the fruit trees in autumn produced an extraordinary crop of fruit. Wasps were in abundance enjoying the sweet juice of the plums. Wooden clothes poles were needed and more borrowed to support the branches of the plum tree, so heavy was the crop. The bottling of the fruit in Kilner jars, and jam making went on for longer than usual, with the shelves in the pantry, step-in press and cupboards were full, leaving little room for the homemade marmalade in January. The talk of the heavy snow and abundance of plums, pears, apples and damsons made a change from the usual conversations of rationing, and of course the war, before, during and after. Interest later that year of the Royal wedding in November, became the next much discussed and anticipated event. Janice's dad was going to be in London at the time of the wedding, at the Dairy Show in Olympia. So, ten thirty on Thursday morning the November 20th, the day of the wedding, Janice was sitting on the big armchair in front of the living room fire, listening to the live broadcast on the wireless. Commentaries inside and outside the Abbey by Colin Snagge, Leslie Mitchell and Geoffrey Sumner and the noise of the crowds went over Janice's head, as she listened very carefully to hear her dad, knowing he was there. The *'man in the wireless'* was also a great mystery, and although she listened to the wireless enjoying many programmes, The Boys of Glen Morach, Life with the Lyons, Ray's a Laugh and Children's Hour just before tea time, she was so disappointed that never once did she see or even find the *'man in the wireless'* who everyone talked about.

Twelve thousand miles away Hector's life was still very much involved with the sea. After leaving the navy and moving back to South Island, the sea and fishing became his life. Around Nelson Bay area, the Tasman Sea and further south to the Parina River, quite unaware that his daughter, though leading a different life, had inherited his love of the sea and boats, and had learnt one Māori phrase, Kia Ora, as Margaret always bought Janice Kia Ora orange juice, explaining to her that her first father was from New Zealand, so she was their little Kiwi.

CHAPTER 26

Return to Paringa – 1998

Search for Truth

The Doctor was pleased and satisfied with Hector's recovery. Driving again, and with no adverse side effects, Hector then asked if he could perhaps try a couple of holes of golf, yes, but nothing too energetic. The smile and positive response cheered Hector up no end, as did the regular faxes and calls from Scotland. There had been no more visits from the Police, which on the surface seemed good, but left lingering questions at the back of his mind as to what the enquiry was really all about. Everything else however, seemed to be slowly getting back to a new normal.

Lynn, Neil's wife's initial call which DSS McIntyre had answered before passing it on to Hector, had said that Neil wasn't fit to have visitors and his progress was slow, adding that he had said he didn't want visitors. Since then, she had not phoned with an update, nor to even to suggest meeting up with her to go to the hospital to visit his stepson.

Hector knew he would have to visit Neil eventually, but instead decided to go back down the river to check the bach, and even retrace and find if he could, where the incident had happened. Perhaps manage to work out what it had all been about, though realising he would need to be very careful not to arouse any suspicion, or worse, have another accident.

Tidying round the house, before organising a few bits and pieces into an old rucksack, he checked the windows were locked, and switches off. Putting a few extra things together like bottles of water, a warm jacket and his waterproof anorak, knowing west coast weather. Looking round outside as he went out to the car, he was pleased there was no one about, no neighbours anyway which was good, no need to explain to anyone where he was going.

Leaving the house and garage secure, he had thought better of it and left a note next door in Jim's letter box, saying he would be back in a few days, he was off to the coast to visit friends. Putting the jackets and rucksack on the back seat carefully, as he had included a gift for his host, he got into the driver's seat. The street was quiet, not even the usual dog walkers out for a morning stroll. Sitting for a few seconds mulling over his plan, though he didn't really have one, but hey, he knew he just had to get himself back over to the coast and have a search around.

He reversed out the drive, the road as quiet as the pavement. Soon he was heading out towards Kaiapoi where Cath and he used to have their strawberry farm years ago after returning from the coast, then on along the coastal road bordering Pegasus Bay at the edge of the South Pacific Ocean. He was enjoying being at the wheel again, taking in all the scenery, in addition to enjoying some music, his favourite, a Welsh male voice choir, and his own company he realised.

Deciding for a change to take the north west route out of Christchurch and head for the Lewis Pass through the Spencer Mountains. Passing through Spring Junction and Reefton, both areas of old gold mines on Route 7, before heading south and west to join route 6 at Greymouth

The road divided further along the coastal route north out of Christchurch to Kaikoura, where he hoped someday soon, he would take his daughter to see the abundant wildlife, the colonies of furry seals, and further out at sea, sperm whales. Today, however, he turned inland towards Culverden, a small town in the northern Canterbury region, lying in the centre of the Amuri Plain. Traditionally surrounded by sheep farms but now due to modern irrigation schemes, dairy farms prevailed.

After a stop to relieve himself and drink some water, he stood admiring a field of cows, before continuing along by the bank of the Hope River and passing the road end to Hanmer Springs. Set below Mount Clara and above Hope River, this was somewhere else he planned he and Janice would visit. More like an Alpine village, though named after the village of Hanmer, Wrexham County Borough, in Wales, in the 1850s by a Thomas Hanmer. Now a year-round holiday spa town with natural hot pools, and stunning landscapes. Ideal for rafting the rapids and jetboats in summer, and with skiing and snowboarding in winter, unless, of course, the roads to it were blocked with snow.

However, no stopping today, Lewis Pass beckoned with the hope of a homecooked meal and a bed for the night at Caitlin and Rhys Hughes's place.

Dreaming was for another day.

He was sure they would be pleased to see him, and in a much better condition this time. Yes, he was much indebted for their help and kindness, so had put a bottle of Johnnie Walker in his rucksack as a 'thank you'.

He made good time by not stopping at Reefton or Greymouth, and was soon heading into Hokitika. Rhys's new Ute was parked by the paddock so that was good luck, a chook might be in the oven, in fact he imagined he could smell it already. He looked at his watch, good timing. He felt fine, not even an ache in his arm or shoulder.

Before he was out the saloon, he heard the welcome committee shouting,

'Kia Ora!' This is a surprise, and a nice one. Hi pehea koe? How is the arm and shoulder? Come on in, dinner is nearly ready, you timed it well, of course!' Caitlin said laughing, 'I'll go and set another place while Rhys helps you with your things. Oh, this is lovely.'

'Yeah, we have been a bit concerned, not having heard from you Hector. Is everything ok?' Rhys asked.

'Sure, fine, everything's sweet. Just need a few days away, so thought I would come over to the coast, maybe even head down the river to check the bach, you know me, never settle in one place for long, always on the go.'

'OK, never mind that just now, let's go in, freshen up, and dinner will be on the table by the time you are ready. Yeah, as Cait says, lovely, great.' And he meant it.

Dipping into his rucksack for the bottle of Johnnie Walker, Hector handed over the bottle of amber nectar, grinning. Rhys shook Hector's hand, then gave him a hug, careful of his arm and shoulder. Both men smiled, awkwardly, but before anything else was said, Caitlin shouted through, 'Dinner is served you jokers, hurry before it gets cold.'

They ate leisurely, savouring every mouthful, then finishing with warm apple tart and melting ice cream. Hector did admit to himself that there was a lot to be said for a well-cooked homemade meal. He still had a bit to learn he realised, and not much time either to improve his skills before his daughter arrived, he thought to himself, as he finished the last mouthful of the delicious sweet.

Early the next morning Hector was up and ready to go before the rest of the house had stirred. Determined to make the most of the day, checking out the bach, seeing if his quad bike was still in one piece, and if his two rifles were intact. It was seeming more than likely there had been some foul play and he had been the target. He was finding it hard to believe, perhaps not wanting to, for the problems it would bring. Catching sight of Caitlin in his rear-view mirror, still in her pyjamas running after him, a bag in her hand, he slowed right down, then stopped.

'Hector wait, wait, I have something for you,' she called. Opening his window as she caught up, she handed in a bag of sandwiches wrapped in foil. 'Take these, I made them last night with some left-over chicken, they'll come in handy.'

'They sure will Cait, you're a great girl looking after this old joker. I'll see you in a couple of days, maybe even tomorrow, depending on how things go, and yeah I'll take more care this time.'

Waving out the open window, he drove off heading south for Ross, where he picked up a bottle of milk and several bottles of beers at the local store, then through HariHari on to Fox Glacier where he and Cath had had the store and tearoom years ago. From there he made his way to the bridge at the head of the river in the hope of catching a lift down to his bach, in Tom the water bailiff's jet boat.

Tom was more than delighted to see Hector, offering him condolences as he hadn't seen him since Cath died, and he had been wondering how he was managing. Hector slipped on his anorak, easiest way to carry it, before they got into the red jetboat and set off. Managing to continue their conversation just, over both the noise of the engine and spray.

'Oh, thanks Tom, you know I am doing fine, a big adjustment, been a bit of a loner most of my life, as you know so not too big a change. I've got golf and fishing, still do a wee bit in the garden and I am pretty adept at falling asleep these days every time I sit down. Seems to come with age I am told. Anyway, just down to check the bach before the weather closes in. I take it none of the old cobbers are about, a bit late in the season now for them I guess, with summer practically over?'

'Yeah, you're right, most away back north or east, even Wayne is away, he'll be sorry he's missed you. Regularly asks after you, and was sorry to hear about Cath. By the way, how is that son of hers? Haven't seen him for a while either. Never too keen on the fishing though, was he? Well, here we are, guess you'll be fine, get me on the CB radio if you need anything. Kia ora.'

Hector thanked Tom and scrambled out the boat on to the stoney banking, carrying his things. Turning to wave, but Tom was already starting up the engine, and turning the wheel to ease round out into the middle of the river to head back up stream. He'd give Tom a call on the radio when he was ready to return. They'd been too busy chatting to plan ahead.

Taking his time picking his way up the stoney beach, and suddenly realising this was his first time down the river to the bach since Cath died, hit him. Aware too it was now his bach, also felt a bit strange, feeling quite sure Cath's west coast family and son, would have different ideas. Dropping his bag on the wooden bench below the corner dual aspect window, he retrieved the key from its usual place under the edge of the stone trough and wiping it. A few of the summer plants in the trough were now struggling to hold their own against the colder wind and rain of approaching autumn. Remembering Cath planting them last September at the beginning of the season, never for a moment thinking it would be their last trip down the coast together. Picking up his rucksack, and walking round to unlock the wooden door, he stood for a moment just inside before closing it and going on in to the living room. Laying his things down on the table by the window, he took off his anorak, hanging it up on its usual peg on the living door, realising quickly, that yes, the old place did seem empty.

First things first, a cup of tea. There was some dry firewood lying in a basket by the stove and a few old newspapers, time to get the fire going. Not only to boil the kettle, but to heat the place up, it felt damp and musty. With the fire crackling away, and the kettle coming to the boil, Hector checked his CB radio up on the old wooden chest of drawers, perhaps he should call Tom later and say all was fine. The tea tasted good, as Caitlin had given him a carton of milk, along with the sandwiches, eating a couple the edge was soon off his hunger. Though tempted, he held back eating them all, as he hadn't as yet checked the freezer to see what was else available, though there should be plenty whitebait for a quick fry up meal. Not Caitlin's standard, but good enough to keep body and soul together under the circumstances.

After checking the toilet and primitive shower that he and Alan had rigged up years before, he pulled his few things out of the rucksack and put them on the bed for later. Although everything seemed fine, the twin beds in the other room too, he did notice one of the two sleeping bags, which usually hung on a rod across the ceiling to air, was lying on top of one of the beds. It hadn't been put back up, odd. Noting this he decided to go outside and have a look around. At first glance all seemed as it should; the two canoes, hanging on their supports from the shed roof, the paddles all in place too, the large boxlike whitebait nets and the buckets as well, his gardening tools, the barrow, all where he left them or thought he had, as best as he could remember. He knew he was putting off, not facing up to why he was really here, the quadbike and more importantly the rifles.

Daylight was fading, and Tom was right, there was no sign of any of the other coasters about. No twinkling lights over the river at Wayne Kelly's place either, or further back along the beach, at either Arthur's bach which looked more like a spaceship, or old Bill's place. He had been hoping to share a Speight this evening with his cobbers, and have a good yarn to take his mind off what was becoming ever clearer, and the real reason why he was here.

Finding plenty whitebait in the freezer from his catch in the spring, he sat some out on a plate near the fire till he was ready to fry it in some leftover oil in a pan on the old stove. It smelt good, and he was hungry, so it would taste good too, which it did. Opening one of the bottles of Speight, he sat at the table by the corner window watching the last of the sun's rays twinkling over the river, the sky first turning pink, then gradually deepening to red out over the Tasman Sea.

A peaceful evening after a long day. Enjoying another Speight, and before turning in earlier than usual in preparation for another early start, Hector wondered how he would deal with whatever he might discover. To take his mind off things he decided to start a letter to Janice, hoping he would remember to post it in Hokitika on his return trip. He found some paper, an envelope and a biro pen in the chest of drawers, but what to say? How did he get into all this mess, and at his age too? Memories of a past love, and gold, that was it, what an old fool, but then there is nothing like an old fool, how true he thought, as he started writing.

All thoughts of calling Tom vanished.

CHAPTER 27

Scotland 1978 – 1998

The Long Wait

Many years after her parents had died, Janice decided to start searching where abouts she had been born, perhaps even find the names of her birth parents. Being a wee Kiwi, she knew New Zealand must hold some clue, though her mother told her not long before she died that her birth mother's family came from Rothesay, on the Isle of Bute.

Clearing out the family bureau she came across a brown envelope with several old birth certificates. One however printed in red and larger than normal turned out to be her adoption certificate, dated and signed in the local Sheriff Court, late 1945. Great excitement, but not many clues. Janice had always had a small birth certificate with her new name, date of birth and Glasgow as place of birth. Armed with the newly found adoption certificate a trip to Register House in Edinburgh was called for; with the hope all would be revealed.

Looking at Janice over his glasses, the clerk said that he was unable to give her, her birth certificate as she had not been born in Scotland. More than a little surprised she asked,

'Well, where was I born?'

'Have you heard of Hexham?' he asked.

'Yes, I think so, it's in Northumberland.'

'Well, you were born near there. You could try contacting the registrar's office in Hexham requesting a copy of your birth certificate. However, as you were adopted, I doubt under English law they would be able to give you your original certificate, but you could try, no harm in asking.' he said, handing back her adoption certificate. Feeling a bit disappointed, but not without some hope and some fresh information, she thanked him.

Later that same summer while on holiday near Dalbeattie Forest, in Dumfries and Galloway on the south west coast of Scotland, a trip to Hexham was decided. Along the A75 to Dumfries, south to the border at Gretna Green and along the A69, the trip took just under two hours. Arriving in Hexham and finding the registry office without much difficulty, they parked nearby. The assistant was pleasant and helpful. Janice gave her date of birth, where she was born, though never mentioning adoption. Shortly the lady returned with the requested birth certificate, and paying the fee, she then handed it over. Thanking the assistant, they left with the precious piece of paper, hardly able to contain their excitement. A cup of coffee in a quiet corner was called for, to absorb the vital, long anticipated information. Dilston Hall, not far from Hexham was where Janice had been born, Lizzie was her mother, married to a CPO in the Royal Navy, yet not the father. Lizzie registering the birth herself the next day, with no mention of an adoption.

All the information was out there, it just took time and patient research to piece it all together. Lizzie had been divorced on the grounds of adultery with the name of Hector Crichton, RNZN 35 The Strand, London. Writing to the New Zealand Embassy in London unfortunately drew a blank. Life went on, but always in the background was the longing to find more. Her name and where she came from, she now knew, the New Zealand connection was not so easy. Eventually searching directory enquiries New Zealand, they found Hector's name and address in Christchurch.

Janice decided to write a letter to her father. Taking her time, she filled him in as best she could about her life, where she lived, her family, and how she had always wondered who and where he was. Adding too, that she never had had any contact with her mother, Lizzie. Eventually picking up the courage to post it, airmail, she waited for a reply, but no reply ever came. Nearly twenty years she waited and by then fifty-three years old, when out of the blue one morning the response came, but not by airmail.

Eleven o'clock one chilly February morning, the phone rang, a piercing ring, and Janice somehow sensed it was for her. Iain answered with his usual cautionary reply.

'Yes, yes, it could be, who wants to know?'

Silence, then, 'A Hector Crichton.'

'A Hector Crichton, well my goodness this is a surprise. Yes, we know his name and yes we have been searching for him, but many years ago. Is he there? OK, so he will phone back tomorrow, that's fine, look forward to hearing from him, and thank you for getting in touch Gayle, this is amazing. Oh, by the way what time is it with you, it is 11.30am here?'

Such was their excitement; they couldn't believe contact had been made after all these years. Janice switched the kettle on. They went through and sat down in the living room, finding it difficult to take it all in. Going back over the years, the wondering, the searching, was it, wasn't it, should we, shouldn't we. The phone's ring cut through their thoughts and conversation.

'Surely it can't be,' said Iain, 'Gayle said he would phone tomorrow.'

Then looking at his watch he realised in New Zealand it was tomorrow, a few minutes after midnight.

'Boy, is he keen!' Iain laughed. 'You had better answer, it's you he wants to speak to, good luck.'

There was no strangeness, no awkward silences, just happy everyday conversation, as if it was one more of many over the years. Phone call followed phone call, fax followed fax, at all hour's day and night. Postcard, followed postcard, scenes of the Southern Alps, Tui birds, rain forests, pancake rocks, of the West Coast furry seals relaxing along the shores of the Tasman Sea. Views of Nelson, of Able Tasman National Park Coastal Tracks and of Christchurch where Hector lived, on the edge of the Pacific Ocean. It was so incredible and so tempting, of course she would travel out to meet him, nothing would stop her. The long time of wondering and waiting was finally over.

CHAPTER 28

Paringa

Revealing Finds

1998

Tossing and turning it was a while before Hector eventually fell asleep. He woke with the dawn. The day was bright and fresh, with a good run on the river. After a bowl of porridge, a slice of toast and jam he found, he washed it down with a mug of warm, sweet, milky tea. Gathering himself together, he checked the kitchen drawer finding his Swiss army knife, a torch and a few other bits and pieces which might come in handy. What he didn't find was the key to the rifle cabinet, nor the key for the quad bike. He shook his head; though wasn't surprised considering all that had emerged recently and which he had been side stepping.

'Hell, what next?' he mumbled to himself.

Flinging on his anorak and picking up his rucksack, he locked the door behind him, putting the key in its usual place. Making his way round to the shed next to the large water tank behind the bach, he noticed the boulder which usually lay up against the door was lying over in the rough grass. Pulling the shed door open, there was just enough light to see that the gun cabinet was lying open, the key still in the lock, a rifle missing, as he had expected. Hector had an idea where he might find it, but it would take a bit of searching. The other wooden shed, nestled under the edge of the trees on the path down to the river banking, housed the quad bike.

The bike more out the shed than in was leaning over to one side, one front wheel and one back wheel damaged and looking as if it had been dragged up the beach out of the way, the drag marks still visible. Putting his rucksack down and using what strength he had, managed to ease the bike further under cover, hopefully away from any prying eyes. Sitting down on a tussock to get his breath back, and rub his arm and shoulder, he thought out his next move.

The initial plan of heading into the bush to find where he had been when the shot hit him, was his first step. So, having taken a few minutes to steady himself, get his breath back and sort out his thoughts, he picked up his rucksack and headed off into the bush. Thankful too that the *Paringa* was quieter than usual, so no chance of bumping into the odd joker down for some quiet fishing, a beer and a yarn.

Climbing now as the sun was, so glad of the cloud cover and canopy of ferns high above him. There was the usual rustle among the ground cover as the odd possum scuttled out of his way. The sounds high in the branches above him, of tuis and bellbirds, like high pitched wind chimes, let him know he was not alone, and being watched. Eventually he reached the ridge, below where he thought he had previously made camp. Glad to sit down on one of the tree stumps after the climb, he had a drink of bottled water and a couple of biscuits, while considering his next move. A few noisy bellbirds fluttered around hoping to share the odd crumb, before flying up into the high branches again to keep an eye on the unfolding scene.

Leaving his rucksack by the tree stump he looked around for a suitable sturdy stick, always handy. Beginning to think he was once again on a wild goose chase, like the gold search which had started it all. He decided to make his way back. At that moment his eye caught something shiny in the undergrowth, Using the stick to move the clumps of grass, the missing rifle was revealed.

Hector couldn't believe he had found his rifle and close by, behind a native Rata tree, a rucksack. Bending down time to pick both up and his stick, a flicker of sun highlighted what looked like a crumpled piece of paper.

'Running out of hands here,' he said to himself. Laying the stick back down, he picked up the damp, crumpled bit of paper, which looked at then put in his anorak pocket. The rucksack over his good shoulder and the rifle in that hand, he picked up his stick before carefully picking his way back to where he had left his own rucksack. His heart was racing, not with exertion, but with the realisation of what he had stumbled upon. The unhappy truth. What was he to do now? Contact Detective Senior Sergeant McIntyre, no, not yet. First the long overdue visit to Christchurch hospital was called for, he knew this for certain, whither he wanted to or not. He needed to face the truth before he finally decided what to do.

First, he had to get back to the bach and sort out what he had found, and wipe any prints off the rifle, before putting it safely back under lock and key. Thinking to himself, others can sort that one out.

By the time he had replaced the now clean rifle and locked the cabinet, and gone back into the bach, pangs of hunger hit him. So before even taking his anorak off he went back outside to the freezer to fetch some whitebait. Never in his wildest dreams did he think when he or Cath put the fish there at the end of last season, he would be scrambling to make a meal with it so soon. or be in this situation. Leaving his meal to defrost, he went down to the other shed to have a better look over the quadbike. Yes, it did need a bit of work but nothing too serious. A quick call to Tom to ask for some help was needed, as between them, he thought, they could manage to get it back up and running.

Though the quick fry-up first was called for. Mana from heaven came to mind as he scraped his plate. Finishing off by taking a piece of buttered bread round his plate to pick up every tiny morsel of whitebait, delicious, and instead of a mug of tea, he enjoyed a beer. Gazing out of the window at the now shadowy *Paringa*, flowing peacefully out to meet the sea as darkness fell, another day was nearly over. However, he needed to make that call.

'Sure Hector, I'll be down the river first light and I'll bring some tools. Yeah, I thought it was your bike. Sorry I didn't manage to get it right under cover, but I was keen to get over to see Wayne after the accident, he was pretty worried, and guess I was pretty shocked myself. See you in the morning.'

Before turning in, Hector looked through the other rucksack, realising there was nothing of importance in it, an empty bottle of water and a paper bag with a few crumbs. He emptied it and put the bag under one of the single beds out of the way. He then had one more thing to check, the crumpled piece of paper, the final piece of the jigsaw. Still in his anorak pocket, he fetched it and laid it on the table, carefully trying to smooth it out as best he could, without tearing it as it was quite damp and dirty. Yes, it was as he thought, a page from original airmail letter from the United Kingdom that had caused the arguments all those years ago. Neil must have found it when he was round at the house recently, when picking up the items of his mother's he wanted. Hector remembering, he had foolishly left it lying on the table along with all the other letters and papers which he had meant to tidy away. Why take that one when there were plenty others from his daughter lying about. Strange that he hadn't missed it.

CHAPTER 29

Help and Confirmation

1998

Up bright and early, having slept reasonably well much to his surprise considering the day he had had. Hector heard the jet boat before he saw Tom. The kettle was on the boil, and a bit of welcome warmth from the woodstove. Pleased he had left a pile of kindling and logs inside the bach at the end of last season; they were certainly coming in handy, that's for sure.

Having beached the craft, Tom picked up his gear and made his way up the shingle to the beach house, and pleased to see smoke curling up out of the chimney. Putting his bag of tools down on the wooden bench, he walked round to the door. Hector greeted him with a hot mug of tea, and the warm glow from the crackling wood stove made him feel additionally welcome. Both men sat at the table over by the window, Hector listening carefully as Tom explained how he had found the quad bike.

Responding to Wayne's call for help, Tom had contacted the rescue team at Hokitika, prior to making his way down the river. Waving across to Wayne, he waited on the helicopter's arrival. After the crew, with Tom's help, had lifted the bike up and off the injured man, the medic examined him, then administered pain relief, allowing them to move him, first on to the stretcher then carrying him along the beach to the helicopter.

Jetting over the river to Wayne's to thank him for his prompt call which set the rescue in motion, Tom then decided to go back over and move the bike as best he could up out of the way nearer the shed, not an easy task. Hector agreed. Later that evening, Tom had contacted Wayne on the CB radio to check he was fine. They had talked over the afternoon's incident with Tom adding that he thought he had recognised the joker who had been injured. Wayne was unable to confirm, having all happened so quickly. and being further away down the river at his nets he was not able to confirm one way or another Tom's thoughts.

After Tom had finished relating what had happened, Hector sighed. 'I think you were right Tom; you did recognise who it was. I have only just found out myself. I got a call from Lynn not long ago to say that Neil was seriously ill in Christchurch hospital, alive, but paralysed it seems. She didn't seem keen for me to go to the hospital, saying Neil wasn't up to having visitors, but she would keep in touch. She hasn't.'

Tom didn't know what to say, apart from how sorry he was to hear that Neil was in such a bad way.

'What puzzles me Hector, is why he was down the river. I checked the your bach after pulling the bike up nearer the shed and found the place secure, so that is why I began to question if it had been Neil. As I said, Wayne was too far away to see who it was, with it all happening so quickly. He was keen to report the accident and get help. Also, if it was Neil, how did he get down the river, I never took him and there were no other coasters about to give him a lift. Strange. Not unless he hiked his way through the bush and forest, and down on to the beach to the bach. Though not an easy hike for someone not used to it.'

After finishing their second mug of tea, they decided it was time to get started on the bike as Tom didn't want to be away from base too long, which Hector understood. Picking up his bag they made their way over to the shed. Tom had brought a couple of combo wrenches, a tape measure and a low-pressure tyre gauge with him, what he thought they would need. The pair worked away, first realigning the handle bars. Measuring the distance needed between the front tyres to about eighty centimetres Tom turning them in slightly again, and then the back tyres to eighty-four centimetres. Checking and tightening any nuts he found loose, he gave the bike another once over, before turning the engine on. It didn't sound too bad. Managing to wheel it back into the shed out of harm's way, Tom then gathered his bits and pieces together, had a quick look round to make sure they hadn't missed anything, before walking back over to the bach, a good job done. Refusing a cup of tea this time saying he would need to get back up the river, Hector thanked him. Both walked down to the river, Hector giving him a hand into the boat with his tool bag, before stepping back to avoid the spray as the jetboat moved off. Hector waved and shouted thanks again. He stood and watched as Tom passed from sight round the first bend, heading on up the five mile stretch to the bridge.

After a bite of lunch, a tin of beans and a slice of toast, washed down by a beer, Hector decided he would call Tom in the early evening to arrange a pickup in the morning, no point hanging around now that he was satisfied the place was in order, rifles secure and the bike, maybe not as good as new, but at least running pretty sweetly. For the rest of the afternoon, he thought he would do a bit of fishing. A while since he had cast a fly, may even catch himself a trout for tea. It might be a while before he would be back down, so best take the opportunity while it was going and hopefully it would take his mind off all that had happened, and why it had happened. Later he would finish his letter to Janice, ready to take out with him in the morning.

CHAPTER 30
A Plan Too Far

Lying amongst the masses of other letters, postcards, bills and advertising leaflets, Neil spotted the airmail envelope, the one his mother had hidden away. He guessed Hector must have found it when he was tidying out Cath's things after she died. Deciding to go into the garden to potter about, leaving Neil to sort out the ornaments, crystal and pieces of his mother's jewellery he wanted, as there was no point in offering to help as it would be looked on as interfering.

Cath's death had been sudden and unexpected, so yes, it had been a great shock and Neil had taken it badly. Hector remembering the day years ago when the letter arrived, and the furious argument which followed. Neil had been tidying out his old room, something his mother had asked him to do many times. Quietly pushing the bedroom door to, but not closing it in the hope they would forget he was there; he listened as he continued sorting out the items he wanted to take with him. Overhearing what was said, the accusations, the anger, and realising how upset his mother had been at his stepfather having a daughter, it was a lot to take in. So, he had step sister, and she had been in touch.

Seeing the dates and postmarks on other envelopes, Neil realised Hector and his daughter were in recent and regular contact. He must have got in touch not long after Cath his mother had died, judging by the dates. Putting the original airmail letter in his anorak pocket, he gathered the cardboard boxes and plastic bags of items he had decided to take back with him and filled the boot of his car. Without bothering to say thank you or see you soon, he reversed out the drive, and headed south out of the city. Hector watched him go, glad he had left Neil to it, as he couldn't have faced another argument over what was bothering him, it was always the same these days.

On the drive home to the small holding and stables south of Ashburton, Neil decided he would tell Hector, he knew about his daughter from Scotland; and that she was not welcome in his mother's house. He knew Cath would not have wanted her there, and he certainly didn't.

Now that Neil had left, Hector decided to finish off the cold ham sandwiches he had made earlier, and a enjoy a couple of the bought sweet cakes. He sat with the tray on his knee and finished off with the bottle of cold Speight. Glancing over and thinking he really should tidy the table, instead he switched on the television to catch the news, but more importantly the cricket results. Zimbabwe national cricket team were touring New Zealand this February and March, playing a two match Test series and five Limited Overs Internationals. He was enjoying the peace of the early evening and catchup of the cricket, which always brought back memories of his own cricketing days at Nelson college, and during the war when over in England, even managing to play at Lords.

Taking his tray into the kitchen he came back, settling down to finish his beer, and was soon snoozing. The sound of the phone woke him with a start. A quick glance at the clock and he knew, someone was up early. After the usual chit-chats, Janice said she was concerned about how he was coping after his wife's recent sudden death, was reassured he was fine. He had the car to go into town to do his shopping, not that he greatly enjoyed that, as he admitted he wasn't a great cook. However, having managed on his own for years, survived living in tents, huts, even caves high in the Southern Alps and on fishing boats, he would manage. He told Janice about being down the *Paringa* river, of how wild and isolated it was, and how he hoped they could go there some day.

He spoke too about his golf, his garden, where he grew silver beet, potatoes, onions, carrots, and also had a couple of lemon trees. In the front garden he grew roses, New Zealand's favourite flower, his favourite too. His pride and joy a bed of pink carpet roses, and two standard rose bushes, Cath's, though not his favourite. He had a display of colourful dahlias and a few 'mums' in the border under the living room window, along with a couple of Birds of Paradise, so yes, his garden kept him busy. Promising to send a few photos fairly soon, as it was still at its best. Realising time was going on, the cost of the call, so talk of Janice coming over to New Zealand would need to be discussed fully another time, both hoping however the visit would be soon. It was a massive step, both agreed, but exciting, a great experience. But there again, such a long way, to the ends of the earth and meeting as virtual strangers.

Putting the phone down and moving over to sit at the table, he opened his map of the west coast starting to plan his own trip to the area where he and Alan had found the small seam of gold many years ago. Always planning to return, but it wasn't to be. Now, seemed as good a time as any, some extra money would certainly come in handy with his daughter coming over, that was for sure. Driving over to Hokitika, parking the car, hiring a flight from one of the local boys he knew, and arranging his return flight three days later from *Gillespies Beach*, it began to feel quite real. He still had his small tent, primus stove, and essentials from years ago, plus a few empty water bottles always at the ready in the garage, so really, he could head off any time.

Pete next door, was in Australia, due back next week he thought, and Jim and Sheila on the other side were visiting family in Auckland, so no one would miss him for a few days. Setting off very early next morning so missing the early city traffic on the 152-mile drive, he headed for *Arthur's Pass* and the coast, and without a stop and light traffic he aimed to be there before midday. This would give him time to park, find and organise the flight with Lewis, hopefully in his small red, Robinson chopper, with no other passengers, It couldn't be better. Giving Lewis his directions, they set off. Sky clear, no wind, perfect. Following the coastal route till reaching *Gillespies Beach*, they turned inland to the Westland National Park. The tops of the Southern Alps white against the blue sky, as they flew over the lower reaches of Fox Glacier before following the winding road till *Mount McFarlane* came into full view. Carefully negotiating the narrow valley between the *Paringa* river rainforest and the foothills of *Mount McFarlane*, Lewis found the landing spot. Helping Hector out with his tent and gear, he wished him good luck with his search, saying he would pick him up in three days' time at *Gillespies Beach* car park, about this time. Watching from a safe distance, the red helicopter climbing up out of the forest clearing, Hector began to wonder if this really was a good idea, especially at his age.

He was sure Alan, wherever he was, would be looking down and shaking his head.

CHAPTER 31

Home and Away Again

Neil deciding on returning home with all the boxes and items, he would go back soon and have it out with his stepfather as Lynn had decided to visit her parents in Timaru, a port city on the eastern Pacific coast for a few days, leaving the stable girl in charge of the horses and the house, as she wasn't sure of Neil's plans regarding the collection of all his mother's possessions. Realising he might at least need couple of trips up and down to Christchurch, and not really wanting to become involved herself, nor ask him to be in charge while she was away, she had asked Jackie to take over. Neil found Lynn's note lying on the kitchen table. Picking it up, his eye caught movement out of the window, it was Jackie with one of the horses in the menage trotting round. After reading the note, he went out to let her know he was back. Jackie cantered over.

'Yeah, hiya Neil, Lynn left instructions for me, regarding feed deliveries and riding lessons, saying too, you would be coming and going as well for a few days. So, yeah Neil, sweet, I'll be fine. I have Lynn's parents' phone number if there are any queries, but I am sure all will be ok.'

'I will be leaving early tomorrow morning Jackie, so will try not to disturb you, though I am sure you will already be up attending to the horses. Lynn is, we are lucky to have you.'

Walking back over to the house and into the kitchen to search the fridge for something to eat, he realised it had been a while since he had eaten anything. Hector had made some cold ham sandwiches for lunch and put a couple of lamingtons from the local baker on a plate which he enjoyed, both washing it all down with a cold beer. Not much had been said between them, Neil was keen to get back to his packing then head home, and this had suited Hector fine.

Up the next morning at the crack of dawn Neil showered, enjoyed some tea and toasted cheese, before flinging his waterproof jacket, hiking boots and a couple of empty water bottles in the back of the car, before looking into the stables to say cheers to Jackie. Driving north on SH1 to Christchurch, one of the most dangerous stretches of road in New Zealand, he was in the city in just over an hour or so, heading on to the coast at New Brighton where his mother used to live. Still finding it odd not to find her at home, he wandered round checking the rooms. Hector was nowhere to be seen, nor his Honda. Neil made himself a mug of coffee, and sitting down at the window table browsed through the paperwork lying there. Letters, postcards, one or two bills, a rough sketch of pathways through the bush behind the bach, leading on to higher ground where he used to go shooting possum with Hector over the years. Several crosses were marked near a small waterfall, where they often rested. Hector enjoyed relating the stories of old goldmines, which in fact were found right up the coast to Ross, on to Reefton at the foot of the Paparoa Range, even east of Westport and on north towards Murchison. Telling Neil too, how he and his cobber Alan always planned to come back some day to search for the seam they had stumbled upon, not far from the waterfall, but they never did, as Alan had been killed in a plane crash taking whitebait out. Although he had been young at the time Neil did remember Alan being killed, as it wasn't long after that Hector and his mother had got together. All had been fine for many years till the fateful day the airmail letter arrived. What a day that had been, he had never seen his mother so angry or distraught, not even when his father died, it still upset him. It was at that moment Neil had an epiphany. He knew where

Hector was, he was hunting for gold. Quickly washing and tidying away his mug, filling two water bottles, picking up the sketch, and putting the airmail letter in his anorak pocket, he headed out, locking the front door behind him.

There was no one around. He knew he could make it to the car park off State Highway 6, not far before the bridge across the *Paringa* by the middle of the afternoon, then hike down the north bank of the river for the good few miles, to the bach. He would take his time, he was in no rush. There had been no heavy rain recently, unusual for the west coast, so the ground underfoot would be less tricky, that was in his favour.

By the time he reached the coast, Neil was beginning to feel very peckish. Deciding to stop off at the small township of Harihari, less chance of running into anyone he knew. The local store/café on Main Street was open, a few of the outside tables already taken, probably with the last of the tourists. Going in, Neil ordered a flat white, from the girl serving at the counter, and two sausage rolls, also a piece of chocolate sponge which had caught his eye.

'Why don't you find a table outside and I'll bring your order out. Shame to miss the view and warm afternoon sun.'

Thanking her, he went out, finding the table at the far end free and away from the rest of the customers. He hadn't too long to wait till the girl appeared and placed his order in front of him, before asking if there was anything else.

'Sure,' said Neil, 'could you wrap up three more sausage rolls please and another slice of your special chocolate sponge cake, that would be great.'

'Yeah, sure, be pleased to, having a shindig?'

Getting no reply, she turned and walked back into the shop to sort out Neil's request. Half an hour later Neil went back in and paid, and collecting his order went on his way.

By passing Franz Joseph Glacier and Fox Glacier car parks, busy with the tail end of tourists and hikers, Neil left the Westland National Park continuing south to the Paringa. Parking his car at the back of the car park under the shelter of some overhanging branches, and away from the few other cars parked there. Changing into his hiking boots and putting his waterproof jacket on, he put his eatables into the rucksack, then lifting his walking stick, always handy in this terrain, he closed and locked his car.

All was quiet, no sound of traffic from the main highway, or from a jet boat on the river. He set off making for the route along the north bank of the river. It had been many years since he had trekked down the river by the trail rather than by jet boat, when Hector used to meet him half way on the quadbike, travelling back to the bach together. Cath, his mother was worried about him walking all that way back from the road himself, usually at school holiday times, after being dropped off at the bridge by one of his older relatives who lived on the coast. Neil always relieved when they arrived at the bach in one piece, feeling it would have been safer and less stressful walking, but never liked to say. Hector had no fear on the bike, or with anything, whereas Neil's fear was real but never liked to show it.

The day was still fine and clear, thanks to an easterly, with clouds high behind him at the head of the valley, the water level too had dropped and was running wide and slow. This part of the trek was all bush, ferns and ancient tree ferns, and unlike other parts of South Westland not too steep or stoney a terrain. The only danger was skirting along the edge of the mostly hidden pathway trying to avoid entanglement in thick roots and even thicker bush. The afternoon sun was struggling to shine through the high tree ferns, yet across the river beneath the beautiful beech forest basking in the sunlight, the water bubbled over the stoney bottoming like a tinkling piano. Neil carefully made his way down on to the stoney beach and along to the bach, it was as if he was the only person in the world. He never saw a possum or heard a bird all the way from the bridge, which had seemed odd.

Finding the key under the stone trough he unlocked the door, went inside, and took his jacket and boots off. Sitting in the old easy chair he closed his eyes and was soon asleep. He was tired, and it had been a while since he had walked so far, never mind on such rough terrain. Waking with daylight starting to fade, he got up and closed the curtains before switching on a light not wanting to attract attention from across the river at Wayne's. He lit his small primus stove out by the covered yard, and made himself a welcome mug of tea before heating a couple of sausage rolls. He was ready for something to eat. The Café/Store at Harihari seemed ages ago, and would be long closed, and Neil long forgotten, hopefully.

However, he hadn't forgotten why he was here. The drive across country earlier in the day, the hike through the bush in the warm sunlight had eased his jealousy, hatred and growing anger. Within only a few weeks of his mother's death, his stepfather had contacted his daughter and it seemed they were now planning to meet here in New Zealand, in his mother's house. There was no way Neil was allowing that to happen. On his return, he would destroy all letters and postcards, nobody need know. Tomorrow morning, he would head for the waterfall, where, as a boy, he and Hector had camped. Hunting for possum and turncoats he remembered, was all about patience. Waiting your chance.

CHAPTER 32

Revenge isn't always Sweet

Tidying up and gathering his few things together, Neil had a last look round, to make sure he hadn't left any telltale signs of his covert visit. It was a warm late summer morning, schools had returned, locals had left the area, leaving only tourists, who seldom ventured this far off the beaten track. Most interested only in visiting Fox Glacier or Franz Joseph Glacier, travelling by helicopter from Hokitika, to land on the glaciers for photo opportunities or walk with a guide to admire the wonderful snow-covered peak of Mount Cook against the usually clear blue sky. There was no sound of the bailiff's jetboat, and all seeming quiet across the Paringa at Wayne's place too. A peaceful morning.

Closing up the beach house and returning the key to its usual place, even though he was coming back, he didn't want to leave anything to chance. Next was the gun cabinet, having taken the key from the dresser drawer, along with the quad bike key, he made his way to the back of the bach, to the shed next to the water tank. He moved the boulder away from the door with his foot, over into the rough grass, and going into the shed he unlocked the gun cabinet. Taking down one of the rifles, he pushed the door to, leaving the key in the cabinet lock. Just something else to lose on his hike, better left till his return. He gathered some ammunition from the box in the drawer under the cabinet, putting it in his jacket pocket. Next for the quadbike in the shed by the edge of the bush on the path down to the river. Gathering everything, he hung his rucksack on the handle bar, and balancing the rifle across the handle bars set off along the beach, avoiding a washed-up tree stump, to the turn off, which eventually led to the scramble up into the rainforest and the waterfall.

Leaving the bike well hidden in the rough bush, Neil made his way up through the forest, listening and watching, for anything unusual. He eventually reached his vantage point, the waterfall well over to his right, the edge of the ridge above where they used to camp was now in sight. He put his rucksack down behind a Rata tree which towered above him and positioned himself flat on his stomach, rifle loaded, aiming the sights at a space between several ancient tree ferns, where Hector, he hoped would be silhouetted against the distant sky.

It all happened so quickly, the sound of the waterfall, and high in the trees the birds disturbed, he saw the familiar silhouette. He took aim and fired. The figure staggered, he fired again, but missed. The man fell with a thud, and never moved. The heavens were an instant cacophony of noise, even the waterfall seemed louder, Neil flung the rifle away, scrambling to his feet, turning and running as best he could, considering the rough ground. His mind racing, and tossing the crumpled page of the letter from his pocket, he made his way back down through the trees, through the bush, stumbling, sweating, oblivious to all the noises of nature around him. He had accomplished what he had come to do. He was free. Now to get back to the bach, leave the bike back at the shed, and lock the rifle cabinet.

'Hell!' he said to himself, 'I left the rifle, God, and the rucksack. Never mind, no one will find them, there will be no one here, the bach is mine now and there are few jokers around at this time of year. I'll sort it all next time I come down.'

Tumbling down out of the bush on to the beach, his caught sight of a figure in the distance further along the river bank on the south side. Reaching the bike, and starting it up, revving loudly, he stared wildly in front of him aiming to get out of sight as quickly as he could. Too late in spotting the washed-up tree trunk this time, the quadbike hit it at full speed. It was the last thing he remembered as he was catapulted into the air, along with the bike. Falling heavily and awkwardly, spine and legs twisted as he hit the stoney beach, the bike partly landing on top of him. Wayne watched in horror from the opposite bank.

S

CHAPTER 33
Complicated Decisions

Tom arrived early as promised. Hector was packed already waiting for him down by the river. He brought Tom up to date about contacting Wayne yesterday evening and promising that next time he was down the Paringa he would come over in his canoe and thank him properly with a dram or two of Johnnie Walker. Adding, that he thought Wayne still sounded quite upset by it all.

Within half an hour or so Hector was thanking Tom once more for all his help, before heading back up the highway north to Hokitika. Deciding to forgo calling in on Rhys and Caitlin, as he wanted to get back home as soon as he could. Deciding he would phone them this evening or possibly when he had some fresh news. Highway 73 was reasonably quiet all the way back, so he made good time. Eventually switching off the music on the radio, to allow his mind to go over what he thought his next move would, or should be.

Turning into the driveway, it felt good to be home. Hector noticed Jim's car was still away, and the carpet roses, though still looking good in spite of the warm dry spell, were in need of some attention. First things first, he picked up his things from the back seat then opened the front door. A couple of pieces of mail lay on the mat, picking them up and after closing the door laid them on the table. He would look at them later, but now for a cup of tea and something to eat. No just a cup of tea, deciding he would head over to the RSA Club for a decent meal, seemed ages since he had had one. A beer and a chat too with some of his old cobbers sounded good, tomorrow he would deal with his latest discoveries.

Morning came quicker than Hector expected. The evening had gone on longer than intended, with more beers too, so his head wasn't as clear as it should have been for the decisions he had to make. He had a lot to think about and sort out, before heading over to Christchurch hospital. Telling himself there was no real rush, and a hearty breakfast was what he really needed to face the day. He switched on the electric ring, put a couple of rashers in the frying pan and just before they were ready, turned the heat down and cracked a couple of eggs in too. It smelt delicious, and hell, he was hungry. While the eggs gently bubbled, he made a pot of tea and set the table adding a couple of slices of bread to his plate. Feeling quite proud of his efforts he was soon tucking in, enjoying every mouthful. His culinary revelries ending with the doorbell ringing.

Detective Senior Sergeant McIntyre and Detective Sands were standing on the doorstep.

'Good morning, Mr Crichton, sorry to disturb you so early, and while you are having your breakfast too, smells delicious. Can we come in; it won't take long?'

Suddenly it didn't taste or smell so delicious, Hector stood back to let his now familiar visitors in. Going over and sitting on their usual seats, Hector hesitated not knowing whither to finish his breakfast, the best bit, soaking up the yolk with the bread, or leaving it. He left it and sat down.

'How can I help you, lucky you caught me, I am going out shortly? I had a late-night last night, so felt a hearty breakfast would do me the world of good before I faced the day, you know how it is?'

'Indeed.' replied the senior officer taking out his notebook. 'We have been round but haven't managed to catch you in, your neighbours too seem to be away. Have you been away Mr Crichton, you are certainly looking much better since our last visit?'

'Yes, I am, and yes, I have, for a couple of days, felt I needed a change. Took myself back over to the coast, to the bach. Unfortunately, none of my old cobbers were around, so it was quiet. I tidied up around the place, cast a few lines, but nothing was biting, so decided I may as well just come back across and sort myself out here, the house, the garden, as I think my daughter from the UK is planning to come over and visit me.'

'You have family in the UK?' surveyed McIntyre, pleased that he hadn't had to bring up the subject.

'Yes, a daughter, she has never been here. I got in touch with her after my wife died. Actually, we have never met, well not since she was a baby. Her mother and I, well the three of us lived in Dunoon, Scotland. She was born early '45 towards the end of the war when Lizzie her mother and I were in Northumberland. I was stationed at Blyth on the east coast of England. RN submarines were patrolling the North Sea to the Arctic Ocean as the German U-boats were by then based in the Norwegian Fjords. Anyway, we returned to Scotland and then after the 6th August, Hiroshima, I was sent back to the Pacific. I never saw my daughter again, just a few photos. Her mother had her adopted by the time I returned in 1948, so that was that. I came back to New Zealand, north island, a shore base, till I left the Navy in 1952. All a long time ago, about fifty-three years.'

'Certainly is.' agreed the Senior officer. 'So, I take it your late wife and her family, well her son anyway, didn't know anything about your daughter, even your life during the war, is that right?

'Yes. It was nearly twenty years after all that, before I met my wife, a widow.'

'I got the feeling previously, that you and your step son didn't see eye to eye. Is this since your wife, his mother died, or before?'

Hector wondered where this was going. He would need to be careful.

'Oh, he heard us arguing one day, ten years or so ago. I had received an airmail letter from the U K and it turned out it was from my daughter. My wife Cath, read it, and yes, the cat was out the bag. I was as surprised as she was, I can tell you. Secretly pleased and hell a bit excited too, I couldn't believe it. Cath on the other hand was angry, unbelievably jealous, always was, and all hell let loose. Neil was visiting and witnessed our argument and his mother's anger. I guess from that day our relationship cooled. Cath hid the letter; and it was never mentioned again.'

'Thank you for being open with us Mr Crichton. Have you been to visit your step son in hospital yet, since receiving the phone call from his wife when we were last here?' DSS McIntyre asked.

'No, I haven't,' Hector replied, 'I didn't feel I would be all that welcome and visitors weren't being encouraged. Maybe it will be different now. In fact, now that I am feeling better having had a few days away, I will make a point of visiting to see how things are, maybe see if there is anything I can do. Now, if there is nothing else, I had better get on. Things to do, and it seems, places to go.'

DSS McIntyre finished writing, nodded to Det Sands and both stood up to go. Heaving a sigh of relief as he watched the officers drive off, he wasn't sure what to make of their visit, so tried to put it from his mind as he started to clear up his now cold and sticky breakfast dishes. Annoyed about missing the warm yolky bread. He put the kettle on again and made himself a fresh cup of tea, it was definitely time to consider his next move.

Phoning the hospital to confirm the visiting hours, he decided to take himself over in the early afternoon, giving himself time afterwards to go to the supermarket for milk, eggs, bread, some fruit and vegetables, as he realised provisions were running low. He was slowly getting into the way of cooking for himself and looking after the house, but along with the garden it was beginning to feel like a full-time job. Hoping too, to get back to the golf, with the weather still fine and his arm and shoulder on the mend. The boys at the club must be wondering what had happened to him. Thoughts of golf, the banter and beer at the nineteenth hole, soon cheered him up.

After showering and changing into a fresh shirt and slacks, Hector set off for the hospital. This wasn't going to be easy, he knew that, but knew he had to look Neil in the eye. What he did or said after that, he still had to work out.

CHAPTER 34
Seeing is Believing

Preparations for the journey to New Zealand were slowly taking shape. First flying to London, Heathrow, then much later that same evening to Changi Airport, Singapore, leaving the following day on an Air New Zealand flight to Christchurch. Quite different from Hector's great grandfather, who as a boy, set sail from Portsmouth in May 1842, spending five months at sea, six weeks becalmed, before sailing safely in to Nelson harbour in the October. Both nevertheless, travelling to an unknown country thousands of miles away, not knowing what to expect.

Janice, was hoping all was fine with Hector having lost his wife recently and not hearing from him, she wondered if he perhaps was having cold feet. Phoning could be awkward with the time difference, whereas writing seemed slow, so she too was beginning to have doubts, exciting though it seemed initially. Sometimes the things you wished for, did not always turn out as you hoped. Unaware of the current situation Hector found himself in, as he hadn't mentioned his accident down the Paringa, nor his returning there to check the place out. Janice would eventually learn how deep and secretive her new found father could be.

As Hector was approaching Christchurch Hospital in Riccarton Avenue on the edge of Hagley Park some twelve thousand miles away, Janice was sleeping, dreaming perhaps of her planned adventure, unaware of the real drama unfolding. Fortunately for once the hospital car park had plenty of empty spaces near the entrance, so walking over and into the open foyer, he remembered hearing, perhaps from Ethel, that this was where his mother Dolly had died, back in 1954. Taking his time, Hector studied the main noticeboard to fathom out which floor the Spinal Traction Unit was on, thinking this is where Neil would be, and hoping Lynn would not be there.

Neil was in safe hands, Lynn knew this, allowing her to catch up at home, helping Jackie with the horses, the stables, and giving riding lessons in the afternoons after school. Driving up later to see her husband and stopping for something to eat in the city before visiting time, made it a long and tiring day. Lynn had never phoned Hector again; also, never told Neil she had phoned him initially about the dreadful accident. Hector did think it a bit strange, but realised she had plenty to do visiting Neil, worrying about his, their future, and running the stables, though he knew she was capable and had good help. Even when Cath was alive there had never been a great bond. Sport being more Hector's thing with the camaraderie involved. Neil and he had watched many a national and international rugby match on TV together, as well as going to Lancaster Park to watch the Crusaders play.

Taking the lift to the second floor he stood for a moment to get his baring before approaching the nurses' station to enquire about his stepson. Staff Nurse Johston, petite, with dark hair and a bright, pleasant face stepped forward and invited Hector into the relative's room.

'Much better having a quiet word in here, we can take our time away from the hubbub of the station.'

Sitting down opposite one another, the Staff Nurse introduced herself saying she had been on duty the day Neil had been brought in to make up staff numbers in A&E. Maia Johnston carefully explained his condition on arrival, the subsequent diagnosis and his present condition. Saying that he was now in a single bedded room in the Spinal Unit ward, explaining his prognosis and his future treatment plan, including daily physio, hopefully in due course leading to his rehabilitation. It was certainly a lot to take in. The Staff Nurse excused herself, returning shortly with two plastic cups of tea and spoons, little pots of milk and several sachets of sugar.

'Thought this might help Mr Crichton. Can't have been easy trying to make sense of it all.'

'Thank you, yeah, a lot as you say. I had no idea it was as bad as it is. Paralysed from the chest down, you are telling me, so Neil will be in a wheelchair from now on? A life sentence really.'

Thoughts rushing round in his head, what to do or say now.

'It will be a long recuperation, with constant physio, but to me he seems a strong guy, determined too, which is good.

'Yeah, he is.' Pausing, Hector inquired, 'Is it alright if I see him Staff Nurse?

'Of course, I'll take you along to his room, then you'll know where to go next time you visit. It was nice talking with you. I am sorry for what has happened; however, I am sure he will make the best of it. Any questions you have, please do not hesitate to ask me or one of the staff. We are here to help.'

The Staff Nurse knocked on the open the door of Neil's room, a few doors along from the relatives' room, saying,

'You have a visitor Neil, I will leave the two of you in peace, but if you need anything just press your buzzer.'

Hector stepped aside to let Staff Nurse Johnston pass, smiling and thanking her. Taking a few steps into the room he glanced round before going forward to the end of the bed. Neil was propped up against several pillows, staring straight ahead, avoiding any eye contact with his visitor. After several moments of uncomfortable silence, and without looking at Hector, Neil eventually said,

'You, it's you, how did you get here?'

'I could say the same,' was the quick reply, 'But unlike you it seems, I got here under my own steam.'

Pausing, staring into Neil's dull eyes, Hector added,

'Surprised to see me? I guess you are, as the last time you saw me was through the sights of a rifle. Didn't think you would be seeing me again, is that right?

The only reaction was the sound of footsteps of a nurse running in, in answer to the emergency buzzer ringing at the nurses' station.

'Everything ok Neil, you rang your buzzer?' asked the young nurse.

'Yeah, everything's ok. My visitor's just leaving.'

Hector continued staring at Neil from the end of the bed, saying nothing he turned and left. He had his answer, but what to do about it was more difficult.

Passing the nurses' station, he looked for Staff Nurse Johnston, but there was no sign of her. He continued along the corridor towards the lift, hoping he might bump into her, but it wasn't to be. Pleased to be out in the fresh air once more he walked over to his car, doubting if being here had actually been one of his brightest ideas. Nevertheless, he knew all he needed to know, the problem now was, what to do next.

'Next?' he said to himself, 'next I have to do some food shopping.'

Driving away from the hospital he headed to the nearest Pak'n'Save, cursing the busy city traffic and hoping his mind would clear allowing him to remember all he needed. Shopping was not his favourite pastime; Cath had always taken charge of that. How things change in the blink of an eye, as he saw today.

CHAPTER 35

Tenacious Time

Arriving home, he noticed Jim's car in the next-door drive. Making note that he would make a point of calling in to see them in the next day or so. First though he had to tidy away the shopping, make a cup of tea and settle down to mull over this morning's visit and decide his next move.

The phone rang clashing with the doorbell. 'Never a moments peace.' he muttered to himself putting his mug down on the coffee table. He answered the door, about to say, 'Come in while I answer the phone', when it stopped ringing. His neighbour Jim was standing on the step.

'Oh, bad timing, sorry Hec,' he apologised.

'Hey, don't worry,' replied Hector, 'whoever it is will phone back, I'm sure, come in. Did you have a nice time, I thought you had been away.'

'Yes, we had. I just wanted to hand in this wee jar of honey from the Honey Centre just north of Auckland, the centre is very interesting. Oh, and before I forget Hector, you had visitors when you were out today. They came round to ask if we knew if you were away from home, or would be back later today. I said I thought you were at home and yes, would be back later. No names, no card, just thanked me and drove off. Couldn't be that important. Anyway, I'll not keep you, but look in soon, be pleased to see you and hear if the honey does have all the magical properties it claimed at the Centre.'

Closing the door Hector sighed, knowing who his visitors had been, card or no calling card, and yes, they would be back.

He poured the now tepid tea down the sink, this was becoming a habit, so instead poured himself a none too chilled beer, having not long come out of his shopping bag. Things weren't going too well.

'Damn, the phone call.' he remembered. Yeah, there was a message, it was from the golf club secretary asking him to call back. What next, he thought, as he slowly appraised the first mouthful of beer. He had bought himself a frozen fish pie for dinner, he would put in the oven later, first to work out how he would tackle the situation regarding his seriously injured stepson.

Neil was certainly in a bad way with the future not looking too bright, though still early days, he knew that. The staff nurse had sounded reasonably optimistic, and though, he would be in a wheelchair, with all the regular physio and massage, he was strong, and yes, there could be a life for him in the outside world. Thinking everything over, he knew it was Neil who had tried to shoot him. His foolish idea had backfired, and as a result he was crippled for life. His target walking free.

Hector put his beer down, went over to the kitchen to switch on the oven, knowing he would feel better after he had eaten. In fact, he was beginning to feel a bit better already, as his head started to clear. The fish pie was tasty and he finished with a slice of apple tart, tinned custard and some of the new Manuka honey drizzled over it. All very nice, he was quite pleased with his cookery efforts this time. After watching the evening news, more importantly the cricket results, and enjoying at last a hot cup of tea undisturbed, he closed his eyes. It must have been an hour later he was roused by the ringing of the telephone. Taking a minute to realise it was his phone, he managed to reach the handset before the caller changed their mind and hung up. Janice was as pleased to hear Hector as he was pleased to speak to her.

Yes, he was fine, and yes, he had had been down the river for a couple of days tidying the bach and the patch of garden, adding it was unusually quiet, as the schools were back, so no holiday makers. Not that there are many as a rule. The local coasters too had gone back home as the fishing season was over. Yes, he had found it a bit lonely without Cath, but he would get used to that. He was more interested to learn if Janice's travel arrangements were still going ahead.

She was wondering when would be a good time, not wanting to upset any plans he might have. After batting a few ideas about, Easter seemed to suit both, neither early nor late this year, so the weather would still be pleasant in South Island and the roads fairly quiet for touring around. Janice would go ahead and sort out flights from the UK via Singapore and let Hector know as soon as the travel arrangements were finalised. Both had a bit of organising to do before the long-awaited, highly anticipated, and now seemingly imminent reunion.

Not only feeling excited about the predicted meeting with his daughter after over fifty years, he knew more importantly he had to organise his thoughts regarding the next visit from the police, which he felt would be soon. Looking at the clock, it wouldn't be today, but feasibly tomorrow, he was sure.

Time to tidy the table and clear away all the paperwork. After all, if he had tidied it away weeks ago, none of this would have happened, and he wouldn't be in this predicament.

CHAPTER 36
Tidying Up

Spending more time, the following morning after breakfast than perhaps he should, he looked through the paperwork gathered on the table. Glancing at, reading, re reading, separating into little piles to be sorted out again and perhaps again. What had to be kept, and what had to be discarded, was not always easy. Condolence cards, along with last year's Christmas cards, this year's birthday cards, a few Scottish postcards, mixed up with advertising leaflets, free offers, a few bills needing attention, pencil written notes, telephone numbers with no names attached, oh dear what a muddle. A cup of tea as usual seemed a good idea, so he put the kettle on for the second time that morning.

Glancing round the kitchen he noted ruefully he hadn't tidied up his breakfast dishes or even those from the previous evening, his excuse being he was too involved with his long overdue tidy out. Hector wanted it cleared away before Jim's aforementioned visitors of yesterday arrived. He found a large empty plastic bag and a couple of empty shoe boxes through in the spare bedroom, ideal for Janice's letters and postcards, and resisted the temptation to read or glance through them yet again. Instead, he put the boxes in his wardrobe drawer beneath several golfing tops. This reminded him he still had a call to make to the Club Secretary, later. He felt much better now that Janice's correspondence was out of the way of prying eyes, as it should have been weeks ago. He knew now, he wouldn't have been in this mess if he had kept things tidy. But hey it was his house, that was how he lived, he didn't know what was going on in other's minds at the time. Hindsight, retrospection, whatever, was indeed a great thing.

As he drank his tea his mind kept drifting back to yesterday's visit to the hospital, and for some reason somewhere in the back of his mind he remembered again this was where his birth mother Dolly had died back in the 1950s; if his memory served him well. He never saw her again after his visit to Durham Street, before he headed off to Littleton Harbour that day to join HMNZS Achilles.

When he returned from the war, he never made the effort to seek her out, why, he didn't really know. He was posted to North Island and came out the navy in 1952, returning to Motueka and would have been at sea, fishing in 1954 when Dolly died. He wouldn't have known about her death till later, perhaps Ethel had told him one time he was home, he couldn't remember. Anyway, yesterday's visit to the hospital had jolted many memories, and few of them were good. It was difficult to begin with, to take in all Staff Nurse Johnston had described, then seeing Neil half lying, half sitting, ashen faced, staring at him in disbelief, eyes vacant, trying to process what he was seeing in front of him, and unable to fathom it. Hector knew immediately, Neil had pulled the trigger.

Too quick, he had taken his eye however briefly, off the target. How often had he told him, shown him, to steady the handgrip with your non firing hand, a light grip, wrist straight, the fingers of your firing hand curled naturally around the handguard. Line up on the side of your dominant eye, the butt firmly in the pocket of your firing shoulder, keeping your trigger finger straight till you are ready to fire. Breathe calmly, relax your body, otherwise you will tire and your accuracy will waver. Never take your eye off the target, then squeeze the trigger.

Yesterday, his dull, cold, empty eyes never left that target.

The sun was over the yardarm, Hector needed a drink, and

certainly not tea. He poured himself a Johnnie Walker, blended in Kilmarnock, near where Janice lived, he had learnt, so would definitely do him good.

Neil was in a bad way he saw that, paralysed from the chest down, the nurse said, never walk again. A life sentence Hector realised, as he had watched him lying there. What good would it do relay all he had worked out that day down the Paringa or at the hospital to the police. Afterall, he hadn't known about the accident with the quad bike. Yes, he had heard a helicopter, that was true, but soon after had blacked out, several times. Jealousy, anger, hatred, Hector realised it now, and understood. No, he would not press charges. He was fine, the flesh wound had healed nicely, sphagnum moss and all.

Neil realised even in his morphine induced pain free state, that Hector knew, he had seen it in his eyes. He knew he was going to have to live with his punishment for the rest of his life, always wondering what his step father really thought, and if he would report him to the police. Hector on the other hand felt his own greed for gold had over taken his common sense. Yes, it had been enjoyable and exciting to contemplate, but in reality, unlikely to materialise, he knew that deep down. The idea of being out alone again in the bush, camping in the rainforest, took him back to younger days, long passed, and yes it would have been a great story to recount to Janice.

The doorbell jolted him out of his musings. Glancing round he removed his whisky glass to the kitchen, placing it behind the ever-increasing pile of dirty dishes, before answering the door. The living room at least was tidy.

Jim standing on the doorstep, caught Hector's look of surprise, as if he had been expecting someone else. 'Sorry to catch you unawares Hector, thought you might like to join us for a light lunch and a pot of coffee, that is if you haven't already had yours. Our daughter Carole dropped off a lemon meringue pie this morning, too much for us, so Sheila thought you might like to join us, being on your own.'

'Very kind of you Jim, yeah, the pie sounds too tempting to refuse. Give me a few minutes to tidy myself, I also have a quick call to make to the golf club, and then I will be over.'

'No sign of your visitors from yesterday then? enquired Jim, 'I thought they might have been over this morning, been keeping an eye out.'

'No Jim, no visitors, can't imagine what it's about, but I am sure they will turn up at some point, if important. Now if you'll forgive me, I'll go and make that call, put on a fresh top, then be over to join you and Sheila. Sweet, I appreciate it.'

The neighbours spent a nice afternoon together, eating and chatting, the couple recalling their trip to North Island, with Hector remembering to mention how good the honey is. He had added some to his apple tart last night for his tea, so a bit early to report any health benefits. They all laughed. The time went in quickly, with Sheila saying she hoped they would do this again, and to make sure if he needed anything he wasn't to hesitate in asking, as this is what neighbours are for, especially now he was on his own. They chatted for a few more minutes out in the front garden, admiring Hector's pink carpet roses which they could just see over their fence. Turning to go back in, they heard and then caught sight of a dark saloon car turning into Hector's drive, just as he reached his front door. They were sure it was the same car and the same couple who had called yesterday.

Both thinking this could cost them another lunch.

CHAPTER 37
Telling All - Nearly

Detective Sen Sgt McIntyre and Detective Sands followed Hector into the living room, sitting in their now usual seats. The DSS took his notebook out of his inside pocket along with a freshly sharpened pencil, Hector noted, then eased himself more comfortably into the chair. Det Sands already seated, was looking round the room as Hector went to fetch three chilled bottles of water out of the fridge, part of yesterday's shopping. Placing them on the coffee table, he then found three glasses. Much easier and less bother than tea he thought, he was learning.

For the first time Det Sands was first to speak, perhaps she had been instructed or was just amazed at seeing the usually untidy table clear of every scrap of paper, and instead had a lacy cloth and a vase of pink garden roses sitting on it.

Hector interrupted, 'As you have noticed I have been busy tidying up, was feeling a bit guilty,' and smiling added, 'though you will also have noticed that I haven't managed to tidy up the kitchen as yet. What with one thing and another, and the neighbours inviting me round for lunch.'

DSS McIntyre quickly surmised that the neighbours had let Hector know they had called round yesterday.

'Well, yes, he did say a man and a woman had enquired after me yesterday, but said he didn't know who they were.'

'Oh, I am sure he would have worked that one out Mr Crichton, I don't think they miss much?'

Taking a mouthful of cold water, Hector savoured the coolness before getting to the point.

'I was visiting my stepson in Christchurch Hospital yesterday. He is certainly in a bad way. Staff Nurse Johnston took me into the relatives' room and explained everything as best she could in layman's terms of course. Neil, being paralysed, no longer be able to walk, and will have a long, difficult road in front of him with his general health too.'

'Did Neil mention the accident, Mr Crichton, by any chance?'

'No, he didn't, actually we never spoke.'

'The main CIB office for the West Coast is in Greymouth, as you will no doubt know, have been in touch with our branch in Christchurch regarding your stepson's accident, asking us to get in touch with you. The accident happened near to your stretch of land down the Paringa, and I believe, involved your quad bike. Is this correct, Mr Crichton?'

'Yeah, it seems my quadbike was involved, I learnt this recently.'

'Yet, you told us a few moments ago that you and your stepson never spoke, so who told you?'

'Well, I put two and two together you could say.'

'Two and two together, you had better explain.' DSS McIntyre said, making himself clear.

Once more sipping some of cool water, and clearing his throat, Hector realised it was now or never.

'Well firstly, the fact that I never heard from Neil again after he had been to the house uplifting all the bits and pieces of his mother's that he wanted, and the disappearance of several items from the garage which he always had his eye on, all seemed a bit strange. Your unexplained visits, not long following my return from the Paringa, coinciding with the eventual and only phone call from Neil's wife about his accident down the Paringa, began to somehow tie things together.'

Pausing for another drink, hector waited till the officer finished writing before continuing.

'I decided once I was fit again, to take myself over to the coast, to check things out. I phoned my friend Tom Connal, the water bailiff, to take me down the river to the bach. We got talking and he said he thought he had recognised the joker who had had the quadbike accident on the bank of the river, but hadn't said as he might have been mistaken. It was one of the other coasters, Wayne Kelly, who lives on the opposite bank, who had seen and reported the accident, but was too far away to recognise anyone. Tom also said he had a feeling it was my quadbike and after the helicopter left to fly to Greymouth with the injured man, he had dragged the bike 'hard yakka', up nearer my shed out of the way, before going over the river to speak to Wayne.

Later that evening after I had checked around my patch and seeing the damage to the bike, I called Tom on the CB and arranged for him to come down the following morning early and between us we could hopefully sort the bike as best we could. This we did, and as everything else was in order in and around the bach, and as none of my old coaster pals were there, I didn't linger. Tom brought me back up to the road the next morning and I headed home. I am sorry about Neil's accident, but why he had been down the river and fooling about I don't know, so I can't help you any further, I am sorry.'

Looking across at Det Sands, who had been quiet but attending closely all through the interview, the DSS nodded, closed and put away his notebook and pencil. Standing and thanking Hector for his time, appreciating too, that he had been very helpful under the difficult circumstances. Adding he would be back in touch at some point to bring him up to date with the proceedings. Closing the door behind them, Hector resisted the temptation to check if Jim was out in his garden keeping an eye on the comings and goings. He went back over to his seat, but before sitting down remembered, and retrieved his glass of amber nectar from behind the dishes. Dishes, well the dishes could wait…again.

'Heavens, is that the time,' he said looking at his watch, 'soon be dinner time.'

Then he remembered he had eaten earlier in the day at Jim's.

'Thank goodness for that, save me putting my chef's hat on. I bet they are really curious now about my visitors.' he said smiling to himself.

Sitting back, he let the whisky slide slowly over his throat and work its magic.

He was reasonably confident with his account to the CIB earlier, certain it would agree with anything Tom would recount if questioned. Thinking over his last trip to the bach, he was sure he had left everything in order. His anorak and golf shirt he had worn on that fateful day he had taken back down with him and burnt in the wood stove. He guessed it would be powder burns the officers would be looking for in a close range shot if he had tripped, as he had described.

Sir Walter Scott's, 'Oh what a tangled web we weave, when first we practice to deceive.' from Nelson College days came to Hector's mind. Yes, it was time to put it all from his mind and look forward. Neil was in the best of care, he had done his best for him over the years and he did understand how he felt about his mother's death, so sudden and unexpected. Perhaps he had taken the law into his own hands, but he felt Neil had suffered enough, and would have to endure a lifetime's punishment. Hector felt it was his time to catch up with his life, a life that would include his new found daughter and family. Long overdue.

CHAPTER 38

1998 - Reunion

The Air New Zealand Boeing 747 touched down at Christchurch Airport on a warm afternoon in early April. Hector and his daughter met at last, in International Arrivals, after fifty-three years. There were no tears, no awkwardness, they held each other's hands, and smiled into each other's eyes. They somehow knew each other.

Refreshing themselves after the long flight from Singapore, then enjoying a light lunch, Janice, her husband Alex, and Hector with three other cousins also descendants of Ethel's. Later they all went out in the Cream Toyota people carrier to the Banks Peninsula, south east of Christchurch. Gazing out over Littleton Harbour to the surrounding blue coloured hills, a magnificent scene, never to be forgotten. This was where Hector had left for war on HMNZS Achilles in 1942/3, and had previously that same day said farewell to his birth mother, Dolly, for the last time. Here he was, here again looking out over the same blue water, this time with his daughter by his side. It was a lot to take in. Never in his wildest dreams could he have imagined this ever happening, Ethel's wish at last had come true.

No matter what the future would hold, it couldn't take this from him. Watching his daughter gazing out over the harbour, he was reminded of his first love Lizzie. Touching his shirt pocket which held his wallet still containing her small, slightly faded, black and white photograph, he smiled to himself, funny how life turns out. Taking a deep breath, he smiled saying, 'Right everyone back to the house, something to eat, then an early night, because tomorrow my daughter, son in law and I, are heading over Arthur's Pass to the coast and on down to the Paringa. We will spend Easter at the bach, fishing and panning for gold at the edge of the Tasman Sea, what could be better?

Two rather tired and stunned travellers, trying to puzzle out where they were in the world, where was north and where was south, as the sun was shining from a different direction. Even the water swirled anti clockwise down the drain in the sink, this was going to take a lot of getting used to. Their searching days however, were over, Edinburgh and Hexham seemed decades if not a lifetime away. Yet looking at one another they realised their adventure was really only now, beginning.

Twenty-four hours later, having slept fitfully, and struggling to know what time of day or night it was, the new little family trio left Christchurch in the people carrier. Crossing the Canterbury plain in bright autumn sunshine, fields of lupins in colourful abundance for miles around as they headed for Arthur's Pass, then on to the coast at Hokitika. Parking as they arrived in town near a local pizzeria, they enjoyed a pizza with a cool drink, before booking in at a local HomeStay. Hector then decided as they were here, they would take a walk to the Glow Worm Dell before turning in for the night. The Dell, located minutes off State Highway 6 in a leafy canyon, of natural limestone caves, was home to thousands of glow worms, a twinkling, magical experience.

Next morning after breakfast they set off for Ross, a small gold-mining town established in the 1960s along route 6, then on through Hari Hari before stopping at Franz Josef to see the breathtaking natural wonder of the glacier of the same name, which still flows almost to sea level. It was here while walking along by the shallow turquoise water's edge of the river valley, that they first experienced sandflies, a biting fly species, which took a great liking for Alex, but certainly not reciprocated. From Franz Josef, they drove thirty minutes south to the town of Fox, tucked away in the forested foothills where Hector had owned the general store and tearoom many years previously, back in the 1960s. Here too is the magnificent Fox glacier, some 300 metres thick of shimmering turquoise and white ice, plummeting some 2,600 metres from high in the Southern Alps, fed by four alpine glaciers along with 30 metres of snow each year. Surface-melting at lower altitudes fed the Fox river down in the valley, before flowing out of rocky ravines, through the rainforests and on out into the Tasman Sea. Later in the week on their way back to Motueka, near Nelson, they stopped off at Fox to experience a helicopter flight up the Glacier, to stand on the ice and wonder at the magnificence of the surrounding mountain peaks including the majestic Mount Cook.

As the afternoon was creeping on, they made their final road trip to the bridge over the Paringa river, parking at Tom Connal's house. Once safely in the jet boat along with their few bits of luggage, Tom started up the engine and off they sped out into the middle of the river. After the first bend and starting to pick up speed to about 50mph, with the spray catching the sun's rays in the western sky, they soon reached their destination. Clambering out of the boat with their bags, Hector already away on up the beach towards the shed to start up the quadbike and trailer, before hurrying back down to the water's edge to collect his dazed family. Tom waved and wished them all well as he curved the jetboat round and sped back up stream.

Hector could hardly believe this was happening, astride his recently sorted bike, his daughter behind him holding on to his shoulders, and his son in law balanced precariously in the trailer with the bags. A short time ago on this same stretch of beach, his stepson lay paralysed under the same quadbike, while he himself lay unconscious in the rainforest, a rescue helicopter flying overhead. Arriving up at his beach house the trio finally stood together looking back at the river with the sun lowering in the sky over the Tasman Sea, away to the west. Hector overcome by this scene, held his daughter's hands, welcoming her to his wooden rainforest home, something he never could have imagined, far less hoped for.

'Welcome home.' he managed to say.

Smiling she replied, 'Thank you, it is quite amazing, never did I dream we would ever meet, and certainly never imagined that if we did, it would be in such a remote, yet beautiful corner of the world.'

CHAPTER 39

Easter 1998

Having spent an uncomfortable, first night in the bach, never having slept in cold, damp sleeping bags before, Janice and Alex were happy when morning dawned. Hector was already up, the woodburning stove crackling a warm welcome, a pot of tea ready on the table by the window, along with three small bowls of porridge.

The plan for the morning was to go down by quad bike and trailer to the sandy beach by the Tasman Sea and pan for gold. In the afternoon a jetboat trip up the river to Lake Paringa, then back in time to cast a line, hopefully catching a fine trout or two for dinner. Janice secretly hoping she would not be asked to gut the trout, although as a child she had watched, fascinated, as her mother carried out this technique expertly over the kitchen sink, many times over the years, after she and her dad had been fishing. Today she certainly had no wish to do so. In fact, this camping type of rough existence, was not really her type of thing she realised, and soon Hector, laughingly, was calling Janice, his 'drawing room daughter!'

Rounding the beach headland at the Tasman Sea, leaving the quadbike up out of harm's way, they walked along the damp sand to a rocky outcrop, home to some curious furry seals. It was a lovely clear morning and though Janice and Alex were still tired and still struggling to realise where they were, they were soon excitedly involved in gold panning. Running in and out of the sea like children, avoiding the small waves rolling up onto the sand. Hector showing Alex how to use the pan in the water, swirling the sand and grit around, before lifting it up and slowly emptying it to reveal a few tiny grains of shining gold. Not enough to get excited about but amazing all the same. This certainly was an adventure and only the first morning.

Jack and Hunter, cousins of Neil's, though Neil's name was never mentioned, arrived by jetboat down from Hunter's bach in the early afternoon, for the promised trip up to the Lake. All five managed into the jetboat and set off up the river at speed. The river narrowing quite soon after they passed under the Highway 6 bridge and headed on inland. The banks on either side were thickly covered with beech trees and bushes, many dipping down, trailing into the water. The afternoon sun reflecting brightly on the river, dazzling the passengers as they sped quickly on towards the lake. Suddenly and without warning, coming towards them on the wrong side of the river was another boat, a speedboat, the sun full in their eyes. Jack swiftly manoeuvred the jetboat over to the left out of the speedboat's way, just in time, before suddenly coming to a sudden halt. The jetboat had become stuck against the trunk of a fallen tree, wedged between the banking and a sandbank. Realising very quickly what had happened, from somewhere at the back of the jetboat Hunter produced a hand power saw. Something you should always have handy in this part of the world it seemed. Hector now lying his length along and over the side of the jetboat, started cutting up the tree trunk to allow the boys to eventually move it out of the way, to allow them to continue upstream and reach their destination.

The lake, usually busy at the height of summer with swimmers and fishermen, was peaceful, allowing the group to relax after their bit of excitement. They now enjoyed a clear view of Mount McFarlane to the south and east and further to the north of the lake, Mount Cook. All quite spectacular. Resting and chatting they headed on back down the river with no incidents, allowing time for Hector to possibly catch a fish as planned, for their dinner. Thanking the boys for the amazing trip Janice and Alex slowly walked back up to the bach, Hector close behind. He picked up the key from its usual place and soon Alex had the fire going and Janice made a pot of tea, as the three mused over their afternoon's exploration and near accident.

Shortly afterwards Hector happily put on his waders and fishing jacket, and picking up his rod was soon heading back down the beach whistling away to himself, not quite believing that his daughter was actually here with him at his favourite place, after all these years. Maybe Ethel was actually looking down and smiling, happy for him. Alan too, thinking his cobber had at last struck gold.

Now to try his luck for dinner. Even before Hector had reached the river, Janice and Alex were both fast asleep, one on the big chair, the other on the old sofa, dead to the world. This new world, which was just opening up to them, only the start, a new beginning.

Two hundred and ninety-one miles away on the east coast, that same afternoon, a man and a young woman arrived at Christchurch Hospital. Parking the car, made their way across and into the bright foyer before taking the stairs to the first floor. They approached the nurses' station.

'Kia Ora, may we speak to the nurse in charge?' the gentleman enquired.

'Yes,' replied Staff Nurse Johnston, smiling, 'I am in charge, how can I help you?'

Showing his warrant card, said, 'We are here to speak to a Neil Crichton; I believe he is a patient here?'

Detective Senior Sargeant Steve McIntyre and Detective Margaret Sands followed the Staff Nurse along the corridor to the relatives' 'Quiet' room.

Would he finally have the answers he had been looking for? DSS McIntyre truly hoped so.

Respectfully Steve said, 'After you Staff Nurse Johnston, and you Detective Sands.' Then he closed the 'Quiet' room door.

In a single room along the same corridor Neil slept, but not for long.

****

ACKNOWLEDGEMENT

I would like to express my profound gratitude to Lex Bloomfield, Steve MacDonald and Alan Young, for their contributions to my research and completion of this latest novel, Ethel.

Printed in Great Britain
by Amazon